Reading & Writing Excellence

KEYS TO STANDARDS-BASED ASSESSMENT

Estelle Kleinman

STECK-VAUGHN
BERRENT

A Harcourt Company

www.steck-vaughn.com

ACKNOWLEDGMENTS

Project Author: Estelle Kleinman

Editorial Manager: Karen Bischoff

Senior Editor: Amy Losi

Editor II: Caren Churchbuilder

Editor I: Edward Nasello

Associate Editor: Christy Yaros

Project Consultant: Howard Berrent

Art Director: Frank Bruno

Design and Production: Susan Geer Associates, Inc.

Designer I: Julene Mays

Design Associate: Gregory Silverman

Cover Design: S. Michelle Wiggins

Photo Research: Sarah Fraser

Illustrators: Eva Cockrille

Eileen Hine

CD Hullinger

Holly Jones

Steck-Vaughn/Berrent is indebted to the following for permission to use material in this book:

page 9 "Abby Takes Her Shot" by Susan M. Dyckman. Copyright © 2001 by Highlights for Children, Inc., Columbus, Ohio.

page 23 "Songs of the Sea" by Catherine Stier. Copyright © 2001 by Highlights for Children, Inc., Columbus, Ohio.

page 30 "I.A.M.M." by Harriett Diller. Copyright © 2000 by Highlights for Children, Inc., Columbus, Ohio.

page 34 "Not Just a Hole in the Ground" by Elizabeth C. McCarron. Copyright © 2000 by Highlights for Children, Inc., Columbus, Ohio.

page 38 "Rory's Funny Story" by Janice Graham. Copyright © 2000 by Highlights for Children, Inc., Columbus, Ohio.

page 46 "A Battle for the Earth" by Sheila Wood Foard. Copyright © 2000 by Highlights for Children, Inc., Columbus, Ohio.

page 50 "Smile for the Camera" by Um Yaqoob. Copyright © 2000 by Highlights for Children, Inc., Columbus, Ohio.

page 58 "A Garden for a Roof" by Mary Houlgate. Reprinted by permission of SPIDER magazine, July 2000, Vol. 7, No. 7, © 2000 by Mary Houglate.

page 64 "Running Rabbit: A Kumeyaay Folktale" retold by Jeannie Beck. Copyright © 2000 by Highlights for Children, Inc., Columbus, Ohio.

page 70 "Alligators Are Really Shy" by Pringle Pipkin. Copyright © 2001 by Highlights for Children, Inc., Columbus, Ohio.

page 82 "The Guest" retold by Uma Krishnaswami. Copyright © 2001 by Highlights for Children, Inc., Columbus, Ohio.

page 90 "The Word Is..." by C.S. Perryess. Copyright © 2000 by Highlights for Children, Inc., Columbus, Ohio.

page 104 "Yaaaaaaawning" by Haleh V. Samiei. This article was originally published in *Muse Magazine* (Dec. 2000 issue).

page 111 "Citizen Carmen" by Fabiola Santiago. Copyright © 2001 by Highlights for Children, Inc., Columbus, Ohio.

page 119 "The Boy King" by Andrea Ross. Reprinted by permission of SPIDER magazine, December 2000, Vol. 7, No. 12, © 2000 by Andrea Ross.

Photo Credits:

p.34 ©Norman O. Tomalin/Bruce Coleman, Inc.; p.46 ©Bettmann/CORBIS; p.58 ©Pat Armstrong/Visuals Unlimited; p.70 ©Joe McDonald/CORBIS; p.71 ©The post and courier/wade spees. 9/10/97; p.105 ©Mary Kate Denny/PhotoEdit, Inc.; p.120 ©Bettmann/CORBIS.

Additional photography by: Corbis.

STECK-VAUGHN
BERRENT
A Harcourt Company

www.steck-vaughn.com

ISBN 0-7398-3953-5

Copyright © 2002 Steck-Vaughn Company

Published by Steck-Vaughn/Berrent Publications, a division of Steck-Vaughn Company.

1 2 3 4 5 6 7 8 9   TPO   05 04 03 02

Table of Contents

Students are instructed to approach a selection and test question using the
Four *R*s: **R**eady, **R**ead, **R**espond, **R**eview.

Unit 1 introduces the three levels of comprehension—literal,
interpretive, and critical—and presents specific strategies designed
to assist students in answering multiple-choice and short-answer
questions. Each question is identified in the instruction by the type
of skill it covers.

Unit 2 explains how students can use graphic organizers to help them
answer essay questions. A graphic organizer accompanies each of six
selections. Students are given instruction in how to use the different
organizers to answer essay questions about the selections. Each
question is identified in the instruction by the type of skill it covers.

Unit 3 builds upon what was taught in the previous two units.
Students apply what they have learned to answer multiple-choice and
open-ended questions about various selections. There are hints to
help them answer each question. Each question is identified in the
hint by the type of skill it covers.

Unit 4 provides students with an opportunity to independently
practice the strategies they have learned. This unit may be used as a
test to assess students' learning and to simulate formal tests.

To the Teacher

Reading & Writing Excellence is a series of instructional books designed to prepare students to take standardized reading tests. It introduces the **Four Rs,** a strategy that will enable students to read selections, understand what they have read, and answer multiple-choice and open-ended questions about the reading material. Special emphasis is given to using graphic organizers as prewriting aids for answering essay questions.

Many genres, such as fiction, nonfiction, poems, fables, and folk tales, are included. Some of the passages are taken from published, authentic literature, reflecting the type of instruction that exists in classrooms today. The questions accompanying each passage represent the different levels of comprehension.

The material in this book provides your students with step-by-step instruction that will maximize their reading success in classroom work as well as in testing situations.

The Four *R*s to Success

People follow plans every day. Plans show you how to put things together or what direction to take. Plans give you steps to follow when you are doing a task.

When you take a reading test, you need a plan that will help you understand a selection and answer questions about it. You can follow this plan by remembering the **Four *R*s:** **R**eady, **R**ead, **R**espond, **R**eview.

Ready Before you read, you need to get ready.

► **Set a purpose for reading** Think about why you are reading. This will help you to focus. If you are reading to answer questions for a test, you will be looking for information. You will also be reading to understand how the different parts of the selection fit together.

► **Preview the selection** When you preview, you look at something ahead of time. Try to find out as much about the selection as you can before you read it. Read the title and look at any pictures. Read any headings. You might even want to quickly read the first paragraph.

► **Make predictions** Next, guess what the selection may be about. This is called making predictions.

Read The next step is to read the selection. You will better understand what you read if you take an active role.

► **Picture what you are reading** For stories, ask yourself, "What will happen next?" Some selections give you information instead. For these, try to figure out what the next part of the selection will be about.

► **Ask questions** As you read, ask yourself questions about things you might not understand. Take the time to guess what the answers might be. Then, reread parts of the selection to see if your answers are right.

► **Check your predictions** Keep your predictions in mind as you read. Are things turning out the way you expected? Make new predictions as you get more information. Keep doing this until you have finished the selection.

Respond

Now you are ready to answer some questions about the selection.

▶ **Read the question** Read each question carefully. If the question has choices, read those, too.

▶ **Think about it** Think about which parts of the selection will help you figure out the answer. Reread those sections. For some questions, you will have to choose the answer. For other questions, you will be writing an answer. Before you write an answer, be sure to organize your thoughts.

▶ **Answer the question** You are now ready to answer the question. For multiple-choice questions, more than one answer often sounds right. Be careful to choose the *best* answer. If you are writing your answer, be sure to include all the points you want to make.

Review

Take another look at your answer. For a multiple-choice question, make sure you picked the best choice. For an answer you wrote, make sure that you have answered all parts of the question. Does your answer make sense? Be sure to check your spelling, punctuation, and grammar.

• • •

UNIT 1

Three Levels of Comprehension

In this unit you will learn how to answer questions at three "key" levels of comprehension.

LEVEL 1: *Find the Key* (Literal Level)

Look for information—At the literal level, you recall or recognize information. The information you need is stated right in the selection.

LEVEL 2: *Turn the Lock* (Interpretive Level)

Determine meaning—At the interpretive level, you use the information in the selection to figure out the answers to questions. You might be explaining meaning. Or, you might be using clues to draw conclusions. For this level, you must show that you understand the information in the selection. You must also know how the different parts fit together.

LEVEL 3: *Open the Door* (Critical Level)

Go beyond the text—At the critical level, you think about the selection and add what you know from your own experiences. You evaluate and extend meaning. You also make judgments about what you have read.

LEVEL 1: Find the Key
Introduction to Literal Questions

A literal question will ask you to recall or recognize information. The answer to the question is found in the selection.

Types of literal questions may include the following:

► Identifying details from the selection

► Identifying the order of events

► Identifying cause-and-effect situations

► Identifying character traits

Identify key words

The key to answering a literal question is to find out where the answer is. Think about where this information might appear in the selection. Then identify key words in the question that might also appear in the selection. For example, look at the following question:

What is the weather like in Brazil?

To answer this question, you would look for the key words *weather* and *Brazil* in the selection. If you cannot find these words, look for words that mean about the same thing. Instead of *weather*, you might look for *climate*. Or, you might look for words that tell about the weather, such as *hot* and *rainy*.

Find the clues

Sometimes you will not have key words to help you. Then you must think carefully about what the question is asking. Look at this question:

Which sentence tells the main idea of the passage?

Here there are no key words to look for, but the answer can still be found in the selection. First, you must know what a *main idea* is. It is the most important idea in the selection. So you would look for the one sentence that clearly tells what the whole selection is about.

Answering Literal Questions

Now you will learn how to answer literal questions about a story. Be sure to follow the **Four *R*s:**

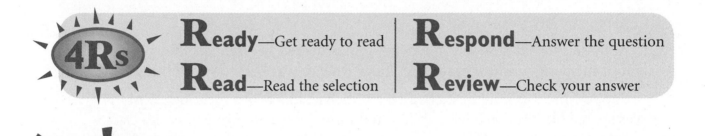

4Rs

Ready—Get ready to read

Read—Read the selection

Respond—Answer the question

Review—Check your answer

DIRECTIONS: Read this story about a girl on a basketball team. Then answer questions I through 8.

Abby Takes Her Shot

by Susan M. Dyckman

A blast of the buzzer ended the game, and the Hawks had won another close one.

"Yes!" shouted Abby, leaping from the bench. Her throat hurt from cheering so hard. The Hawks were undefeated after thirteen games—the best record a Willow Grove Middle School team had ever had.

Not that Abby had made much of a contribution. Her playing time totaled only about ten minutes for the entire season. It didn't help when her brother Michael teased her as she walked toward the locker room. "You're a cheerleader in a basketball uniform," he said. "All you need are pompoms."

Abby felt Mom's eyes on her from the bleachers. Abby forced a little wave, but her eyes stung from tears. She ducked into the bathroom before joining Coach McKenzie and her teammates.

Coach was all smiles. "Girls, your defense was awesome," she said. "And Kathy, your free-throw shooting helped a lot. Nice game."

Abby felt like shouting, "My free-throw shooting could help, too—if I could just get in the game!" She thought of the hours she'd spent practicing. Foul shots, lay-ups, dribbling.

Mom said it was worth it. Abby was a fifth-grader and she'd made the team.

Made it through two rounds of cuts during the tryouts. But Abby quickly learned that making the team and playing in the games were two different things.

Mom was waiting in the car. Abby blinked back tears as she opened the door. She knew Mom wanted her to succeed as much as Abby wanted to herself.

"Are you OK?" Mom asked.

Abby swallowed hard and nodded. Mom squeezed her hand as they pulled out of the parking lot. Mom always knew when it was best to say nothing.

Suppertime was quiet. Dad had taken Michael to a Scout meeting, so Abby was spared her brother's teasing. She and Mom talked about next week's class trip to the aquarium. After clearing the table, Abby went to her room to do her homework.

When she'd finished, Abby grabbed her basketball and raced downstairs. As she flicked on the outdoor lights, Mom came up behind her. "Want some company?" she asked.

"I guess," Abby answered.

Mom took her spot under the basket. Abby always led off their "make it, take it" games.

"I know what you're going to say," Abby began. "I made the team and I should be happy."

"Not this time, Abby," Mom said. She passed the ball back, and Abby hit her second jump shot in a row. "I just want to say that I'm proud of you for hanging in there."

Abby's next shot bounced off the rim. Mom grabbed the ball and dribbled back to the free-throw line.

"What time is your game on Saturday?" Mom asked as she shot.

"Ten-thirty," Abby said. She grabbed the rebound. She held the ball tightly and looked at Mom. "I really thought I'd play more. Even in fifth grade."

"I know you did, honey." Mom put her arms around Abby and hugged her tight. "Your time will come."

The gym was packed for Saturday's game, the last one of the season. The lead seesawed back and forth, and the Hawks' starters were breathing hard at halftime. Coach McKenzie was encouraging. "Stick to your game," she said. "Work the ball around until you get an open shot."

The crowd cheered as the second half began. Abby watched intently as the players ran up and down the court. The score remained close, and the Hawks trailed by one point in the final minute.

"Come on, Hawks," Abby breathed. A few seconds later, Kathy stole the ball and raced toward the basket. As she went up for the shot, an opponent slammed into her, knocking her to the floor. Kathy did not get up. The gym got very quiet as Coach McKenzie and the trainer checked her ankle.

Finally, Kathy was helped to the bench. She would be all right, but she definitely was not going back into the game.

The referee came over to the bench. "Coach, you need a sub at the free-throw line. She gets two shots."

Coach looked at the players on the bench. She'd always stressed the importance of free-throw shooting. Who had paid attention? Kathy, for one. And . . . Abby. She hadn't played much this season, but she certainly could shoot.

"Abby," Coach said. "You're in."

Abby's stomach flipped. "Me?" she said. "Now?"

Coach stepped closer to her. "I've watched you in practice," she said. "You can do this."

Abby jumped up, reported in at the scorer's table, and walked to the line.

She glanced at the scoreboard. Two points and a few seconds of defense would win the game. The referee handed Abby the ball. She took a deep breath. Two bounces. She crouched and let the ball fly.

Swish.

The crowd roared.

"One more," Abby thought. She caught the ball. Bounce, bounce. Shoot.

The gym exploded with cheers as the ball went through the hoop. Seconds later the buzzer sounded. The Hawks were undefeated. Abby's time had come.

DIRECTIONS: Read each question carefully. Darken the circle at the bottom of the page or write your answer on the lines.

I   What grade is Abby in?

A   Fourth grade

B   Fifth grade

C   Sixth grade

D   Seventh grade

Find the Key

This question asks you to identify details from the story. Read the question and the answer choices carefully. The answer to this question is right in the story. Think about where the answer might be found and go back to this part of the story. When you go back to the story to find the answer, look for a form of the key word *grade*. Once you have found the answer, you can make your choice.

2   Abby's mother is proud of her because—

F   she has stayed on the team

G   she has played in every game

H   she has made many free-throws

J   she has explained her feelings to her coach

Find the Key

This is a cause and effect question. The effect is that Abby's mother is proud of her. What is the cause? Why is she proud of Abby? Skim the story to find the part where Abby and her mother talk. Then look for the word *proud*. Choose the answer choice that says why Abby's mother is proud of her.

Answers

1 Ⓐ Ⓑ Ⓒ Ⓓ	2 Ⓕ Ⓖ Ⓗ Ⓙ

3 Which event in the story happened *first*?

   A Kathy was knocked to the floor.

   B Abby made two free-throw shots.

   C Mom joined Abby as she practiced.

   D Coach put Abby in the game.

Find the Key

This question asks you to put events in the order in which they happened. You probably have a good idea of the order just from reading the story. Go back and find each event in the story. Then put the events in order. Which event was the first to happen?

4 Why did Coach McKenzie choose Abby to make the free-throw shots?

   F She did not want Abby to feel bad.

   G Abby was the only player left on the team.

   H She knew Abby could shoot well.

   J Abby raised her hand and asked to shoot.

Find the Key

This question asks you to identify details. Start by eliminating any answers you know are wrong. Then, to find the right answer, reread the part of the story where Coach chooses Abby. What does Coach think of as she is deciding who will make the free-throw shots? What does she say to Abby when Abby is unsure?

Answers

3 Ⓐ Ⓑ Ⓒ Ⓓ	**4** Ⓕ Ⓖ Ⓗ Ⓙ

5 Why does Abby feel like crying at the beginning of the story?

_____

_____

_____

_____

Find the Key

This is another cause and effect question. For this question, you will write your own answer to the question instead of choosing an answer. Read the question carefully. Then reread the beginning of the story. This is where you will find the answer. Think about why Abby is not happy that her team has won the game. What was she thinking? Write your answer in a complete sentence.

6 What is the setting for the second half of the story?

_____

_____

_____

_____

Find the Key

The setting of a story is where and when it takes place. Here, you are asked to tell the setting of the second half of the story. In the first half, Abby sits on a bench while her team plays a game and then goes home with her family. Where and when does the second half of the story take place? The answer is right in the story. Be sure to write your answer in a complete sentence.

7 How are Abby and Kathy alike?

_____

_____

_____

_____

Find the Key

This question asks you to compare the two characters. The answer is right in the story. Kathy is mentioned in the second half of the story. Go back and reread the section where Kathy is mentioned. What is it that Kathy and Abby have in common?

8 At the end of the story, it says that "Abby's time had come." What does this mean? How does Abby's time come?

_____

_____

_____

_____

Find the Key

This question asks you to identify details from the story. Reread the end of the story. What finally happens to make Abby's time come? Think about what Abby does at the end of the story and why this is important.

LEVEL 2: Turn the Lock
Introduction to Interpretive Questions

A detective looks at different pieces of information to find answers.
When you answer an interpretive question, you put together different
pieces of a selection to determine its meaning.

Types of interpretive questions may include the following:

▶ Interpreting character traits

▶ Interpreting vocabulary

▶ Determining the main idea

▶ Summarizing information

▶ Drawing conclusions

Unlock the answer

To answer an interpretive question, you must become a detective. Before a
detective can look for clues, he or she must know what to look for. You can
tell what to look for by examining the question.

Suppose you had to answer a question about *Beauty and the Beast,* a story in
which a beautiful young woman falls in love with a beast. Look at the
following question:

Why does the young woman fall in love with the beast?

The answer will not be right there in the story for you to find. You have to
think carefully about what you have read to figure it out. You would need to
reread the parts where the young woman and the beast talk to each other.
How does the beast act toward the young woman throughout the story?

Put the clues together

After you have reread parts of the selection, think about what you have read.
Then, like a detective, put the clues together to draw a conclusion.

In the question above, you might find that the beast was kind and gentle with
the young woman. Perhaps they shared things in common. These clues show
you that the woman could overlook the beast's appearance and fall in love
with his inner self.

Answering Interpretive Questions

Now you will learn how to answer interpretive questions about a poem.
Remember to follow the **Four Rs**:

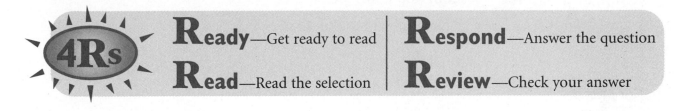

4Rs

Ready—Get ready to read | **R**espond—Answer the question

Read—Read the selection | **R**eview—Check your answer

DIRECTIONS: Read this poem about two young animals. Then answer
questions I through 6.

They Didn't Think

by Phoebe Cary

Once a trap was baited
With a piece of cheese;
It tickled so a little mouse,
It almost made him sneeze.
An old rat said, "There's danger,
Be careful where you go!"
"Nonsense!" said the other,
"I don't think you know!"
So he walked in boldly—
Nobody in sight;
First he took a nibble,
Then he took a bite;
Close the trap together
Snapped as quick as wink,
Catching mousey fast there,
'Cause he didn't think.

Once there was a robin,
Lived outside the door,
Who wanted to go inside
And hop upon the floor.
"No, no," said the mother,
"You must stay with me;
Little birds are safest
Sitting in a tree."
"I don't care," said Robin,
And gave his tail a *fling*,
"I don't think the old folks
Know quite everything."
Down he flew, and Kitty seized him
Before he'd time to blink;
"Oh," he cried, "I'm sorry,
But I just didn't think."

DIRECTIONS: Read each question carefully. Darken the circle at the bottom of the page or write your answer on the lines.

1 Which word best describes *both* the little mouse and the young robin?

A funny

B smart

C careless

D shy

Turn the Lock

This question asks you to compare the two animals. The answer is NOT in the poem. You must figure it out. Think about what happens to each animal. What does the mouse do? How would you describe his behavior? What does the robin do? How is his behavior like that of the mouse? Now look at each choice. Are the two animals funny? Are they smart? Do you think they are careless? Are they shy?

2 What does the word *fling* mean in the poem?

F break

G click

H look

J toss

Turn the Lock

This is a vocabulary question. The word *fling* may be new to you. Have you ever heard it used before? Reread the part of the poem that has this word. Does this give you any clues to the word's meaning? How is the robin acting? What do you think he would most likely do with his tail?

Answers

1 Ⓐ Ⓑ Ⓒ Ⓓ	2 Ⓕ Ⓖ Ⓗ Ⓙ

3 Which sentence *best* states the theme of this poem?

   A Think before you act.

   B Be kind to others.

   C Do not give up.

   D Always tell the truth.

Turn the Lock

A theme is a lesson or message the author wants to give the reader. Most often, the author does not state the theme. The reader must look at the clues and figure it out. To find the theme of this poem, think about what happens to the two young animals. What are they warned about? What do they do? What happens to them?

4 If this poem needed a new title, the *best* choice would be—

   F "Catching a Mouse"

   G "The Foolish Pair"

   H "Birds Should Stay in Trees"

   J "Staying Safe"

Turn the Lock

The title of a poem usually tells the main idea of the poem. The main idea is what the poem is mostly about. Notice how the title of this poem, "They Didn't Think," tells what the poem is about. Look at the answer choices. Find another title that tells the main idea of the poem. Remember that the poem is about both the mouse and the robin. The title must refer to both of these animals.

Answers

3 Ⓐ Ⓑ Ⓒ Ⓓ	4 Ⓕ Ⓖ Ⓗ Ⓙ

5 Summarize the poem in a few sentences.

_____

_____

_____

_____

Turn the Lock

When you summarize, you tell only the main points and important details. To summarize this poem, ask yourself these questions: What is most important about what happens to the mouse? What is most important about what happens to the robin? What details could be left out?

6 Why do the older animals in the poem give the younger animals advice?

_____

_____

_____

_____

Turn the Lock

This question asks you to draw a conclusion about something. Think about what the older animals say to the younger animals. What does the old rat say to the little mouse? What does the mother robin say to the baby robin? Why do the older animals know about such things?

LEVEL 3: Open the Door
Introduction to Critical Questions

For a critical question, you must go beyond the words on the page. You bring in your own experiences to evaluate and extend meaning. You also make judgments about what you have read.

Types of critical questions may include the following:

▶ Analyzing the situation

▶ Predicting outcomes

▶ Determining the author's purpose

▶ Extending the passage

▶ Evaluating the passage

Step through the door

Now, you are going to become a judge. You will still look for clues to answer a question. But you will also study the information, decide how important it is, and make judgments about it.

Let's go back to the story *Beauty and the Beast.* Look at this question:

**Do you think that a woman could actually fall in love
with an ugly-looking beast? Why or why not?**

There is no way to find the answer in the story. Even putting together clues will not give you the answer. This question is asking for your opinion. You must make a judgment based on the story and on your own experiences.

Make a case

A judge never makes a hasty decision, and neither should you. Think about the people you love. Why do you love them? Are your feelings based on what they look like?

Next think about the story. Even though it is a fairy tale, are the characters believable? Do you think that the young woman could fall in love with the beast?

Form your opinion and make a judgment in order to answer the question.

Answering Critical Questions

Now you will learn how to answer critical questions about two passages.
Don't forget to follow the **Four Rs:**

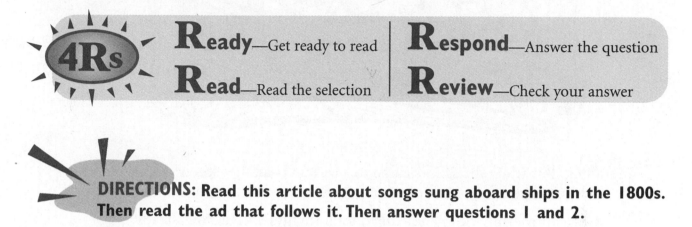

Ready—Get ready to read   **R**espond—Answer the question

Read—Read the selection   **R**eview—Check your answer

DIRECTIONS: Read this article about songs sung aboard ships in the 1800s. Then read the ad that follows it. Then answer questions 1 and 2.

Songs of the Sea

by Catherine Stier

You have signed on for months of hard work. You're far from home. The pay is bad. The food is worse. You find rare comfort in the simple songs that you and your work mates sing.

This is what a sailor's life was like in the 1800s. The songs sung aboard ships were called *sea shanties* (also spelled *chanteys*). You have probably heard a shanty or two yourself. Many of these songs have lasted through the years. They can often be found in surprising places today.

Sea Shanties Then . . .

Sea shanties were valuable friends to sailors. Some shanties, such as "Blow the Man Down," had lively words and melodies. They broke up the boredom of long trips. Other shanties, including one called "Oh, Shenandoah," had a sadder tone. They helped seafarers express longing and loneliness. Still other shanties, such as "Leave Her, Johnny," let sailors grumble about their hard lives.

But the first job of the sea shanty was to help the men work as a team. Ships had sails that were controlled by a system of moving ropes. For many jobs, all of the sailors had to tug on the ropes at once.

When faced with such a job, the *shantyman*, or song leader, began a tune. The crew joined in on the chorus, and it might have sounded like a playful

sing-along. But when the sailors came to a certain beat, they knew it was the signal to pull together with all of their might.

Raising or lowering the anchor called for a rhythm with a slow, steady motion. Then, the shantyman would choose a shanty with a slow, steady beat to match the job. Each duty on the sailing ship had its own rhythm and its own kind of song.

. . . and Sea Shanties Now

Sea shanties have been passed down to us in much the same way as folk stories. Long ago, someone came up with a memorable idea and melody. Others repeated the shanty, often adding changes along the way.

Over time, people saw the sea shanty for the treasure it was. Like any treasure, shanties were collected. Many were written down in books.

Where do the old shanties pop up now? Today's musical artists love the fun, beauty, and history of these songs. Many musicians, including Bob Dylan and Harry Belafonte, have their own versions of "Oh, Shenandoah." One group, the Robert Shaw Chorale, recorded a collection of shanties.

In Hollywood, shanties serve as a symbol of the sea. A fisherman sings the shanty "Spanish Ladies" in the film *Jaws*. The cartoon character Woody Woodpecker whistles "Blow the Man Down" when he finds himself aboard a pirate's ship.

Today, shanties tell us about shipboard life more than one hundred years ago. They help us understand what the working sailor sang and perhaps thought about.

So the next time you're doing a boring task, try making up a tune to go along with it. Time may pass more quickly, and your job may seem easier. Also, you may understand why sailors loved those old songs of the sea.

Seaside Recordings proudly presents

Jack Shaw's latest CD—

Sea Shanties

Explore the musical history of sailors and whalers through their songs. The shanties on *Sea Shanties* are a musical looking glass into the past. The words in the shanties tell how sailors lived long ago.

Jack Shaw has created a truly unusual CD. *Sea Shanties* both entertains and informs. The music in the songs is enchanting. The words are informative. A delightful introduction teaches readers about the history of shanties. The CD also offers explanations of and reasons for each song.

The CD has over 21 songs—over an hour of music! *Sea Shanties* lets you listen to famous melodies that you've heard since you were a child. These tunes will make you feel as if you are actually on the high seas.

To order *Sea Shanties*, fill out the form below. Please include your check or money order made out to Seaside Recordings. Allow 6 to 8 weeks for delivery.

Yes! I want to order *Sea Shanties*. Please send me ___ CDs for $17.95 each.

Name _____

Address_____

City _____ State _____ ZIP _____

Phone _____

Mail this form to Seaside Recordings, 564 Jackson Avenue, Palo Alto, CA 94301.

DIRECTIONS: Read each question carefully. Then write your answer in a paragraph on the lines.

1   Why do you think people still listen to sea shanties?

_____

_____

_____

_____

_____

_____

_____

Open the Door

This question asks you to extend the meaning of the passages, or go beyond them. The first thing you have to do is look back at the article to find reasons why people still listen to sea shanties. It is a good idea to list the reasons as you find them. You will find some reasons right in the article and in the ad. Also try to come up with one or two reasons of your own. Tell your reasons in a few complete sentences.

2 Advertisements usually try to persuade people to buy something. Do you think that the advertisement for *Sea Shanties* will persuade people to buy the CD? Why or why not? Write a few sentences explaining your answer.

_____

_____

_____

_____

_____

_____

_____

Open the Door

This question asks you to predict what will happen. First, you need to find places in the ad where the author tries to persuade readers. Go back and reread the ad. Underline or jot down any persuasive sentences. Then, write a sentence or two explaining whether you think what the author says will persuade readers to buy *Sea Shanties*.

Speak Out

You have read how sea shanties made the work of the sailor easier. Think about how music made a task you had to do easier. Prepare a short speech about your experience. Then give your speech to the class.

Summary

In this unit, you have learned how to answer questions at three "key" levels of comprehension.

Find the Key	*Turn the Lock*	*Open the Door*

"Literal"	**"Interpretive"**	**"Critical"**
Look for information	*Determine meaning*	*Go beyond the text*

Remember that no matter what type of question you answer, you should always use the **Four *R*s:** **R**eady, **R**ead, **R**espond, **R**eview.

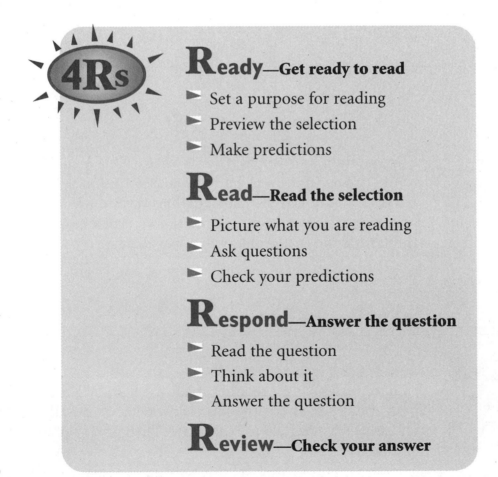

4Rs

Ready—**Get ready to read**
- Set a purpose for reading
- Preview the selection
- Make predictions

Read—**Read the selection**
- Picture what you are reading
- Ask questions
- Check your predictions

Respond—**Answer the question**
- Read the question
- Think about it
- Answer the question

Review—**Check your answer**

Graphic Organizers: The Key to Answering Essay Questions

The Essay Question

In Unit 1 you answered both multiple-choice and short-answer questions. Another type of test question is an essay question. For an essay question, you must write a few paragraphs. Essay questions often require more thought than other types of questions. You must recall and understand details of the passage you just read.

Get Organized!

You know how hard it is to find something in a messy drawer. You look and look, but the thing you are looking for escapes you in the clutter. However, finding something in a well-organized drawer is very easy. In the same way, you can answer an essay question more easily if you are organized before you begin to write.

A **graphic organizer** is a picture that lets you put your ideas in order. A graphic organizer helps you gather the information you need to answer your essay question. Once you organize your thoughts and ideas, it will be easier for you to write your essay.

In this unit, you will learn how to use different kinds of graphic organizers to answer essay questions. But first, here are some things to think about before you begin to write.

Before You Write

Before you write anything, ask yourself some questions:

1. *What is my topic?* What will you be writing about? State the topic in a few words. This will help you focus your writing.

2. *Why am I writing?* Think about the purpose of the essay. Usually you write to explain something, persuade someone, entertain someone, or describe something.

3. *Who will read my writing?* This is your audience. Your teacher will probably be your audience for a test.

DIRECTIONS: Read the following story about a girl named Dorsi who likes to put things off. Then you will use a Character Traits Web. It will help you choose two words that best describe Dorsi.

I.A.M.M.
by Harriett Diller

Mom didn't like the idea at all.

"Why do you have to keep those mealworms in the refrigerator, Dorsi?" she asked.

"Mom, my lizard's got to eat."

"But why can't your lizard eat lukewarm mealworms?"

"Because they have to be refrigerated or they'll rot." Not pretty but true.

"At least put them on the high shelf and in the back," Mom said. "Away from you-know-who."

You-know-who is my little brother, Travis. "In a minute, Mom," I said.

When I say, "In a minute, Mom," that means I'll do it—sometime. Of course that sometime might be in the next century.

"Come on, Travis," I said. "Help me feed my lizard."

Travis likes helping. There's only one thing he likes better. Cooking. His version of cooking, anyway. His favorite recipe is stone soup. He got the idea from this book Mom reads to him. Only instead of stones, he uses blocks for stone soup.

After we fed my lizard, Mom called us to the supper table.

"Have you moved that container yet?" Mom asked me.

"No, Mom," I said, dishing up another helping of green-bean casserole. "Don't worry. He won't get it."

"But I might grab the wrong container and—what if I told you that those crunchy things on top of the green beans aren't really onions?"

I stopped chewing. "That's not funny, Mom."

She turned to Travis. "Travis, that bread doesn't belong in your milk cup."

"Me cook," Travis said with a big smile. "Dorsi eat."

I pretended to eat what Travis had "cooked" and told him, "Yum-yum good."

"Yum-yum good," he said, stirring the glop in his glass.

Later that night I watched TV while Mom put Travis to bed. Then Mom came into the family room.

"Finally," she said, dropping into a chair. "I had to wait until Travis's stone soup finished cooking before he'd go to sleep."

"Why didn't you tell him to put it in the crock pot again?"

"I tried," she said. "He didn't fall for it this time. Listen, Dorsi. About those mealworms. You need to move them A.S.A.P."

Mom thinks I'm supposed to do everything A.S.A.P. (As Soon As Possible). I think I.A.M.M. (In A Minute, Mom) is soon enough. "As soon as this is over."

But by the time the show was over, we'd both forgotten about the mealworms. The next morning I opened the refrigerator and reached for the container to get a couple of mealworms for my lizard.

"They're gone!"

"Who?"

"My mealworms."

Mom and I stared at the container from Marsha's Pet Shop, which was open and empty.

"Travis!" we both yelled at the same time.

Travis was sitting on the floor in his room stirring something in a big plastic cup from Shakes to Go.

"Yum-yum good."

"Travis," said Mom. "What is that?"

"A shake. Yum-yum good." Travis went right on stirring.

I worked up my courage and looked into the cup. There is no word horrible enough to describe what was in there.

"Dorsi drink," Travis said.

I backed away. "It stinks!"

"Travis," said Mom, "show me where you got this milkshake."

"Yum-yum good."

We followed him to the kitchen. Of course he opened the refrigerator. Of course he pointed to the mealworm container.

"He made a mealworm milkshake," I cried. If only I'd moved the container A.S.A.P. to the high shelf as Mom had said.

Mom poured the you-know-what down the garbage disposal. It made a horrible stink going down.

That afternoon I bought more mealworms at Marsha's Pet Store.

"Dorsi, you'll put those mealworms somewhere Travis won't get them?" Mom said.

"A.S.A.P., Mom." This time I hid them at the back of the top shelf behind the horseradish. Out of sight, out of reach, out of mind. At least I hoped so.

Travis went back to making stone soup. Which is a big improvement over you-know-what. I'd rather eat stone soup any day. Yum-yum good.

The Character Traits Web

A **Character Traits Web** helps you organize your thoughts about what a character is like. In this organizer, the name of the character goes in the center box. A character trait (a word that describes the character) goes on each line coming off the center. Then, follow each trait to the box with the word *Example*. Here you write an example of how the character shows that trait.

Read the essay question and instructions on page 33.

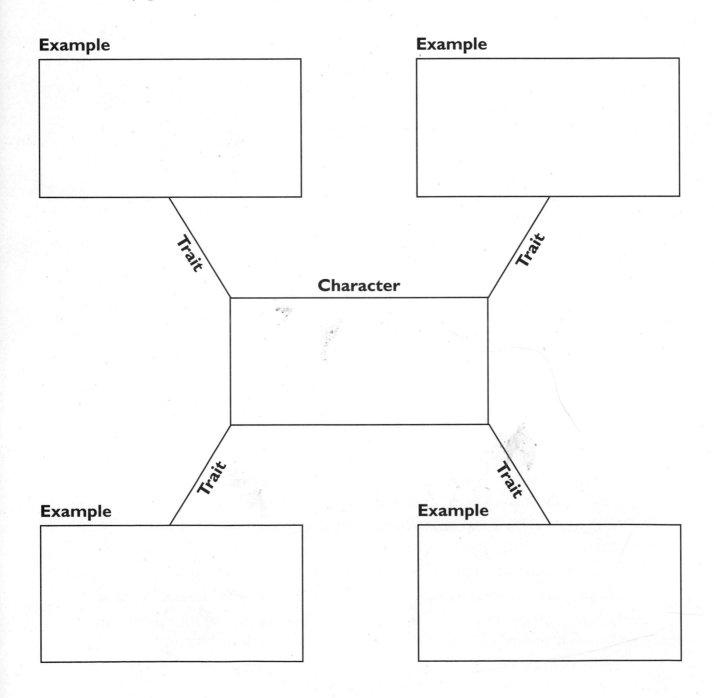

Example

Example

Trait

Trait

Character

Trait

Trait

Example

Example

Essay Question: Choose two words that you think *best* describe Dorsi. Then use an example from the story to explain why you chose each word.

1. You must choose two words that *best* describe Dorsi. Since Dorsi is the character you will be writing about, write her name in the center box of the Character Traits Web.

2. Next, write a character trait on each of the four lines extending from the center box. A character trait is a word that describes a character. To help you think of some words that describe Dorsi, look back at the things she says, thinks, and does in the story.

3. Now follow each trait up or down to its Example box. Go back to the passage to find an example of how Dorsi shows that trait. Then write this example in the box.

Now you have four words that describe Dorsi along with examples. Choose the *best* two. Use them to answer the essay question at the top of the page. Write your answer on a separate sheet of paper.

Open the Door

This question asks you to analyze a character, or tell what you think of her, by describing character traits. This is a critical question. You must go beyond the text and make a judgment about what you have read.

Look at the graphic organizer you just filled in. Choose two of the traits on the organizer to write about. Write about each trait in a separate paragraph. Include an example from the graphic organizer for each trait.

Don't forget the fourth *R* in the **Four *R*s:** **R**eady, **R**ead, **R**espond, **R**eview. Make sure that your writing is the best it can be. To do this, use the checklist on page 56.

DIRECTIONS: Read the following article about a woodchuck's home. Then you will use a Main Idea Map. It will help you explain why a woodchuck burrow is a perfect place for an animal to live.

Not Just a Hole in the Ground

by Elizabeth C. McCarron

The woodchuck sits up on its hind legs, chewing a wild strawberry. Looking around, the chuck freezes when it spies the farmer's dog. The dog sniffs the air, spots the chuck, and charges toward it. The woodchuck watches the enemy coming closer and closer, then POOF! The chuck disappears from sight, and the dog is left puzzled. The woodchuck has dropped into its burrow to escape.

A woodchuck burrow is more than just a hole in the ground. It is a complex system of entrances, tunnels, and rooms called *chambers*. Burrows give woodchucks a place to sleep, raise young, and escape enemies. When a woodchuck *hibernates* (sleeps through the winter), it makes a simple burrow and plugs the entrance with sand.

A woodchuck uses its strong claws to dig its own burrow. In soft soil, a woodchuck can dig an entire burrow in one day.

Each summer burrow usually has several entrances. This lets the woodchuck roam and still have a safe hole nearby in case danger comes along.

For the main entrance, a chuck may choose the woods at the edge of a meadow. The hole must be hidden from view but close to food.

The *plunge hole* is a special burrow entrance. It goes straight down two or more feet. When an enemy comes near, the woodchuck may give a shrill whistle, then drop straight down into the hole. This is how the woodchuck "disappeared" from the dog's sight!

Under the ground, tunnels and chambers connect the entrances. There is a sleeping chamber, a turnaround chamber, and a nursery chamber. A woodchuck burrow can even have a bathroom! A woodchuck may bury its waste in a chamber. Sometimes it adds waste to the mound of sand that marks the main entrance. This mound lets other animals know whether or not a burrow is *active* (being used).

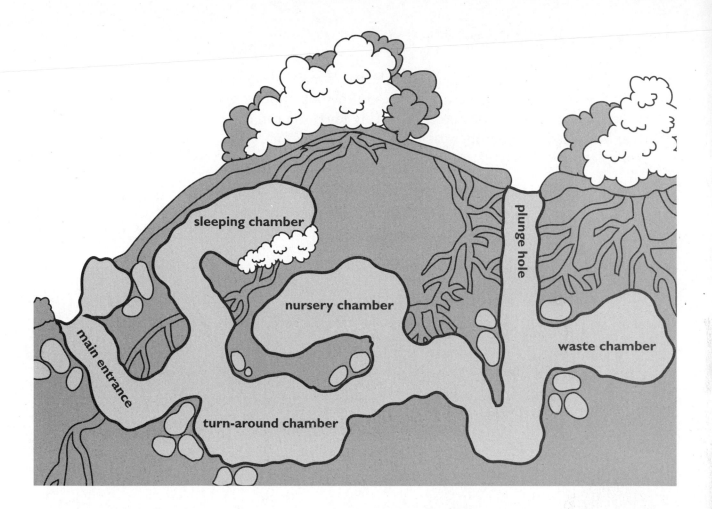

Many animals look for empty woodchuck burrows. And why not? The burrows are warm in winter, cool in summer, and ready-made. Rabbits use empty burrows to avoid summer heat. They may even pop into an active burrow to escape an enemy. Skunks, weasels, and opossums use empty burrows as woodchucks do—for sleeping, hiding, and raising their young. Foxes may take over active burrows to raise their own young in the warm dens.

Now you can see that a burrow is more than just a hole in the ground. It's the perfect place for woodchucks—or other animals—to sleep, hide, and raise young. To a woodchuck, there's no place like its burrow!

Main Idea Map

A **Main Idea Map** helps you organize a selection's main idea, or what it is all about. In this organizer, the main idea goes in the box at the top. Under the box is a circle for each subtopic, or supporting idea. You can add as many circles as you need. Then, under each subtopic is a box for details about the subtopic.

Read the essay question and instructions on page 37.

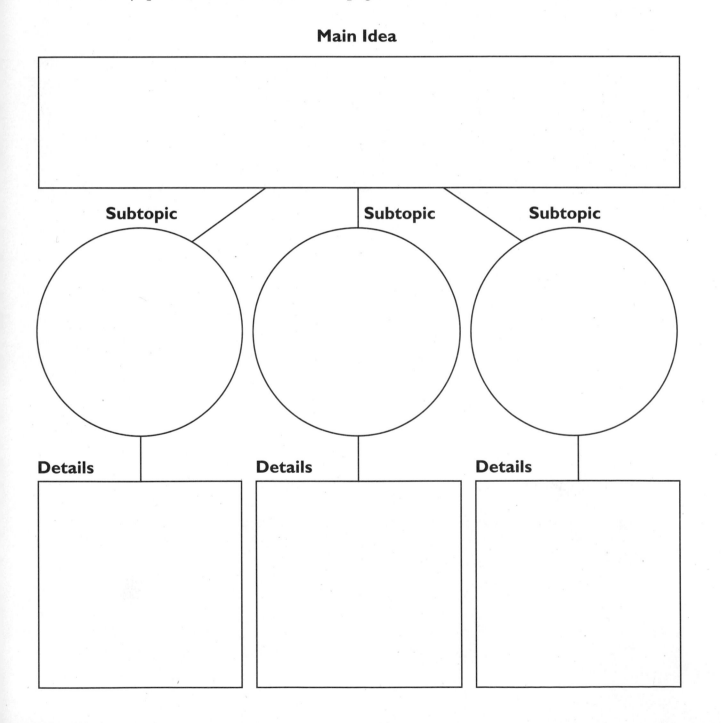

Main Idea

Subtopic   **Subtopic**   **Subtopic**

Details   **Details**   **Details**

Essay Question: Why is a woodchuck burrow a "perfect place" for an animal to live? Use details and examples from the article to support your answer.

1. This question already gives you the main idea: "A woodchuck burrow is a perfect place for an animal to live." Write this as the main idea in the box at the top.

2. Next, you have to find the subtopics. Why is the burrow a perfect place for animals? Reread the last paragraph of the article to find the subtopics. One of the subtopics is "to sleep." Write this in the left subtopic circle. Then fill in the other two subtopic circles.

3. Now look for details on each subtopic. These go in the box under the subtopic. Under the subtopic "to sleep," you might list "has a sleeping chamber" as one detail. Continue to fill in the details for each subtopic.

Now that you have filled in the **Main Idea Map,** use it to answer the essay question at the top of the page. Write your answer on a separate sheet of paper.

Turn the Lock

This question asks you to summarize what you have read about by identifying the main idea and supporting details. This is an interpretive question. You must look for clues. Then put all of your clues together to reach a conclusion.

The question gives you the main idea: "A woodchuck burrow is a perfect place for an animal to live." You need to discuss why it is the perfect place to live. Start your essay by stating the main idea. Then give the subtopics and details from the graphic organizer.

Remember to **Review**. When you are done, make sure that your writing is the best it can be by using the checklist on page 56.

DIRECTIONS: Read the following story about a boy with some funny stories to tell. Then you will use a Sequence Map. It will help you write about Rory's weekend.

Rory's Funny Story

by Janice Graham

Everybody in Rory's class had a Funny-but-True story to tell. The teacher, Mrs. Evans, had the best Funny-but-True stories of all. On Monday she told about her cat playing the piano. On Tuesday she told how she found a nibbled-on piece of bologna in the toe of her red high-heeled shoe. On Wednesday she told about a mysterious truck dumping a mountain of rocks in her driveway. The neighborhood kids climbed and played on it until the truck came back to move the mountain to the right address.

Mrs. Evans had a million funny stories. But Rory couldn't think of even one to tell.

"It's time again for our Funny-but-True stories," announced Mrs. Evans on Thursday. "Who has one today?"

Rory slumped in his chair.

"I have a Funny-but-True!" cried Dana, waving wildly. "My big sister lost her new diamond engagement ring. She was really worried. My mom looked in all the places my sister had been. And there it was in a basket of laundry, sparkling in the dirty socks!"

The class smiled, and some people chuckled. Rory leaned forward and plopped his chin on his desk. Nothing funny ever happened to him.

Friday's Funny-but-True was the best one yet. Tad told how his sister had found a hairy black tarantula the size of her hand in the bathroom medicine chest. After she was through screaming her head off, she decided to keep the spider for a pet. Rory sighed. The class would laugh about that one all through lunch recess. Somewhere in his life there had to be one Funny-but-True story. But Rory knew his weekend would be just the same old boring thing.

Rory's dad promised they would try out the new dome tent in the backyard Friday night. "Just my luck," thought Rory when a lightening storm blew up. He shuffled into the house to find his dad had turned it into a campground. The new tent filled up the living room like a big blue elephant. "What next?" thought Rory.

On Saturday, Rory's four-year-old sister decided to see if her baby bunny could swim. Just in time Rory saved the soggy bunny from a bucket of water.

While mom gently blow-dried the little rabbit, he explained to his sister that bunnies can't swim. "Silly kid," thought Rory.

On Sunday Rory and his family piled into the car and headed for Grandma's house. Passing drivers stared and pointed. When they got there, Rory discovered that their cat, Tiger, had ridden to Grandma's on the roof of the car. "Dumb cat," thought Rory.

"Time for Funny-but-Trues!" said Mrs. Evans on Monday. Rory looked around the room. He was sure Dana or Tad had another great story, but nobody spoke up.

"Rory, how about you?" asked Mrs. Evans.

Rory shook his head. "Nothing funny ever happens to me."

"Oh, I bet funny things happen all the time," said Mrs. Evans. "Tell us about your weekend."

Rory told about sleeping in a tent in the living room. The class looked surprised. He saw a few smiles. Next he told about the bunny's swimming lessons. A few people giggled. When he told about Tiger riding on the roof of the car all the way to Grandma's house, the class broke into roars of laughter.

Rory tried, but he couldn't stop laughing either.

Sequence Map

Sequence is the order in which events happen. A **Sequence Map** shows you the order of the events in a story. In this organizer, there is a group of boxes joined by arrows. The first event goes in the first box, the second event goes in the second box, and so on. You can use as many boxes as you need. Next to each box is an oval. Here you write the details about each event.

Read the essay question and instructions on page 41.

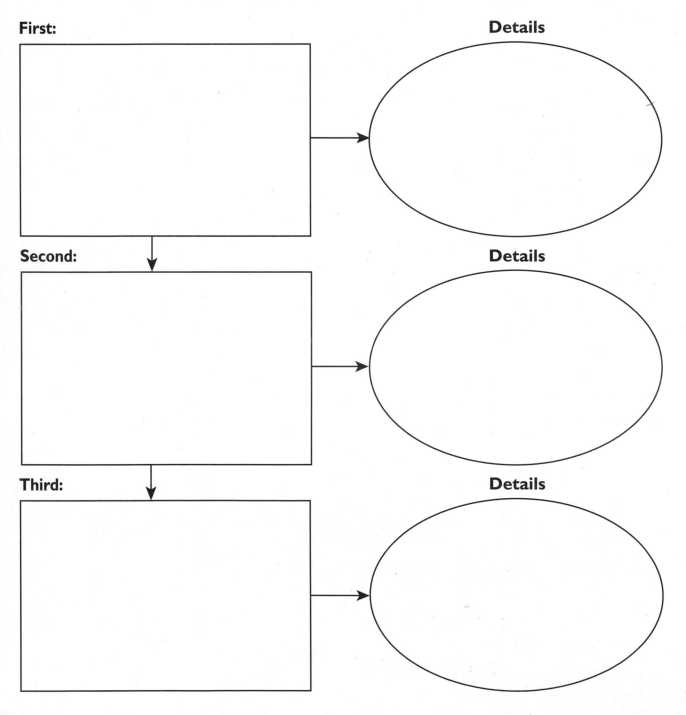

First:

Details

Second:

Details

Third:

Details

Essay Question: Imagine that you are Rory. Write what you told your class about your "Funny-but-True" weekend.

1. The Sequence Map will help you put Rory's weekend in the correct order. Look back at the story. What happened on Friday night? Write this event in the first box at the top. Then write the details of this event in the oval to the right of the box.

2. Next, look back to find out what happened on Saturday. This is the second event. Write it in the second box. Then write the details of this event in the oval to the right of the box.

3. Lastly, write about what happened on Sunday in the third box. Then write the details in the oval to the right of the box.

Now that you have filled in the **Sequence Map,** use it to answer the essay question at the top of the page. Write your answer on a separate sheet of paper.

Turn the Lock

This question asks you to summarize the story by listing the order of events in the story. This is an interpretive question. You must gather clues.

Look at each event on the graphic organizer and the details about it. Think about how you would tell these events if you were talking to the class as Rory. Then, write your essay. Write a paragraph for each event.

Remember the fourth *R*. After you finish, use the checklist on page 56 to review your writing.

DIRECTIONS: Read the following poem about a silly conversation between a father and son. Then you will use a Venn Diagram. It will help you write about Father William when he was young and when he was old.

Father William

by Lewis Carroll

"You are old, Father William," the young man said,

"And your hair has become very white;

And yet you **incessantly** stand on your head—

Do you think, at your age, it is right?"

incessantly = constantly

"In my youth," Father William replied to his son,

"I feared it might injure the brain;

But now that I'm perfectly sure I have none,

Why, I do it again and again."

"You are old," said the youth, "as I mentioned before,

And have grown most uncommonly fat;

Yet you turn a back-somersault in at the door—

Pray what is the reason for that?"

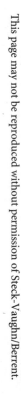

"In my youth," said the sage, as he shook his grey locks,

"I kept all my limbs very supple

By the use of this ointment—one shilling a box—

Allow me to sell you a couple?"

"You are old," said the youth, "and your jaws are too weak

For anything tougher than **suet**;

Yet you finished the goose,

with the bones and the beak—

Pray, how did you manage to do it?"

suet = animal fat

   "In my youth," said his father, "I took to the law,

   And argued each case with my wife;

   And the muscular strength which it gave to my jaw

   Has lasted the rest of my life."

"You are old," said the youth; "one would hardly suppose

That your eye was as steady as ever;

Yet you balanced an eel on the end of your nose—

What made you so awfully clever?"

   "I have answered three questions, and that is enough,"

   Said his father, "Don't give yourself airs!

   Do you think I can listen all day to such stuff?

   Be off, or I'll kick you downstairs!"

Venn Diagram

A **Venn Diagram** helps you describe how two things are alike and how they are different. In this organizer, there are two overlapping ovals. The name of each of the things being compared goes at the top of each oval. The ways the two things are different go in the *outside* parts of the ovals, the parts that do not overlap. The ways they are alike go in the middle *overlapping* part.

Read the essay question and instructions on page 45.

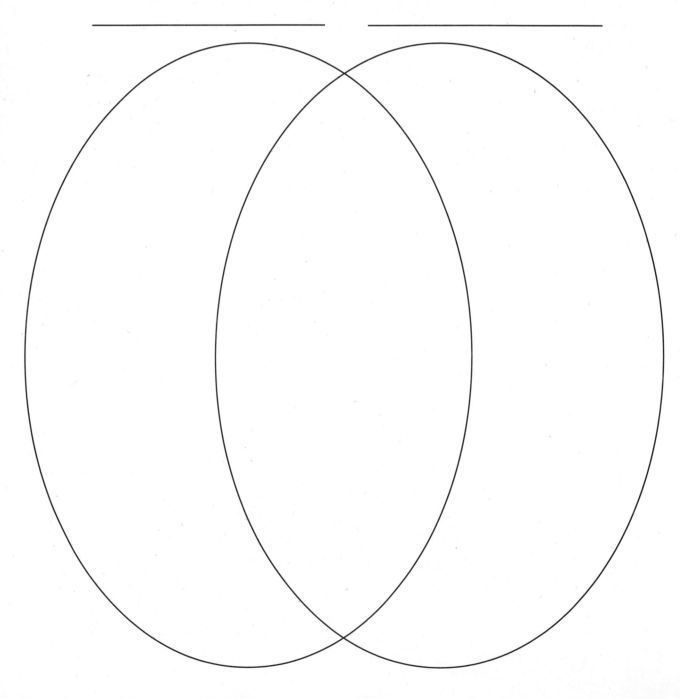

Essay Question: How is Father William different now from the way he was when he was young? How is he the same? Use details from the poem to explain your answer.

1. The essay question asks you to compare Father William when he was young to the way he is as an old man. On the line at the top of the first oval, write "Young Father William." On the top line of the second oval, write "Old Father William."

2. Next, read the poem for clues to tell you what Father William was like in his youth. Reread the poem and think about the way Father William is now. Write the ways in which he is different in the outside part of the oval. Details of how he was in his youth go in the first oval. Details of how he is as an old man go in the second oval.

3. Now think about how Father William has remained the same over time. What things can he still do now that he was able to do in his youth? Write how he has stayed the same in the middle *overlapping* part of the ovals.

Now that you have filled in the **Venn Diagram,** use it to answer the essay question at the top of the page. Write your answer on a separate sheet of paper.

Turn the Lock

This question asks you to compare and contrast information about Father William by identifying details in the poem. This is also an interpretive question. Remember that you must gather details and reach a conclusion about these details.

Look at the graphic organizer. Use the details on your graphic organizer to write your essay. Write about the way Father William has changed and how he has remained the same. Then try to reach a conclusion about Father William. Think about whether Father William has changed a great deal or only a little.

4Rs   Remember to **Review**. Check your writing on page 56.

DIRECTIONS: Read the following article about a scientist named Rachel Carson. Then you will use a Cause and Effect Map. It will help you explain why Rachel wrote a certain book and what the book achieved.

A Battle for the Earth

by Sheila Wood Foard

When she was ten years old, Rachel Carson knew she wanted to write. But why wait until she grew up? Her favorite magazine printed stories by children. She would send one in. If only she had a story to tell . . .

The year was 1918. The United States was at war. Rachel's brother, Robert, had joined the army a year earlier. When he sent letters home, Rachel's mother read them aloud. One letter told of a pilot whose plane had been shot.

Was this a story Rachel could write about? She listened carefully. One wing had been damaged. The plane would crash unless the pilot acted quickly. He climbed out and inched along the wing. The pilot held on like an acrobat and balanced the plane again. His copilot landed it safely.

This was it. Rachel had an exciting story to tell. She wrote about that pilot in her own words, then sent in her story. Five months later, she opened *St. Nicholas* magazine and felt a thrill. Her name appeared under the title "A Battle in the Clouds."

Rachel kept writing. *St. Nicholas* printed more of her work. Her poems and essays won awards at school.

At college, Rachel studied English. But in her third year, she focused more on science. As a young girl, Rachel had loved the wildlife and plants in the fields around her home. Now, in her science classes, she enjoyed studying those animals and plants.

Rachel became a *biologist*, a scientist who studies life and living creatures. She wrote about what she learned. Her three books about the sea became best sellers. Rachel was able to combine her love of science with her love of writing.

In 1958, Rachel received an alarming letter from a friend. A poison had been sprayed to kill pest insects, but many birds died, too. That *pesticide*, or pest killer, was known as DDT. Just as her brother's letter had once inspired her to write a story, Rachel again had a story to tell.

First, Rachel collected facts from scientists around the world. She learned that DDT and other pesticides had helped to control some harmful insects that carry diseases. However, they had also killed harmless insects, fish, and birds. Even our national bird, the bald eagle, was dying out. Pesticides were polluting the earth and poisoning humans, too.

Rachel wrote a new book called *Silent Spring*. She said that people must be more careful with pesticides, or else there would be no birds left to sing in springtime. She wanted scientists to seek less harmful ways of controlling pests.

When *Silent Spring* came out in 1962, many people did not believe what Rachel had written. She waged a battle of words to convince them—a battle for the earth. She showed courage, like the war hero whose story she had written long ago.

Rachel appeared on television. She spoke in front of many groups of people, including lawmakers. In time Rachel gained support from people around the world. They shared her concern for cleaning up the earth. Laws were passed to stop the use of DDT, and people joined groups to protect the environment.

Rachel Carson died in 1964. Today she is remembered as a great *environmentalist*, a person who searches for ways to protect nature in an ever more crowded world.

Cause and Effect Map

A *cause* tells you why something happened. An *effect* is what happened as a result. A **Cause and Effect Map** helps you organize causes and effects. In this organizer, there are two pairs of boxes. Each pair is connected with an arrow. The first box in each pair is for a cause. The second box is for its effect. You can add as many boxes as you need, depending on the passage.

Read the essay question and instructions on page 49.

Cause   **Effect**

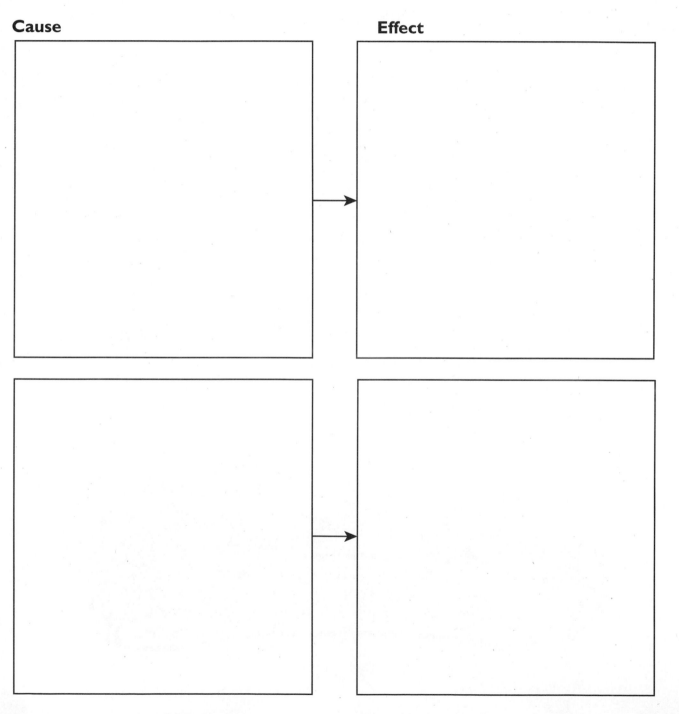

Essay question: Imagine that you are Rachel Carson. In a letter to a friend, tell why you wrote *Silent Spring* and what it achieved.

1. To answer this question, you need to know two things: (1) why Rachel Carson wrote *Silent Spring* and (2) how people reacted to the book. Go back and reread the part of the passage that discusses *Silent Spring*. Then look at the first pair of boxes. In the *Effect* box on the right, write "Rachel Carson wrote Silent Spring." Then list the reasons why she wrote *Silent Spring* in the *Cause* box on the left.

2. Next, write "Silent Spring was published" in the *Cause* box on the left. Then write how people reacted to the book in the *Effect* box on the right.

Now that you have filled in the **Cause and Effect Map,** use it to answer the essay question at the top of the page. Write your answer on a separate sheet of paper.

Turn the Lock

This is a cause-and-effect question in which you must identify details from the article. It is an interpretive question. You must put together different pieces of the passage to determine its meaning.

Use the graphic organizer to help you write your letter. Write as if you were Rachel Carson. In the first paragraph, explain why you wrote *Silent Spring*. In the second paragraph, tell what you achieved by writing *Silent Spring*.

4Rs Remember to **Review**. When you are done, check your writing on page 56.

Speak Out

You have read how Rachel Carson fought to protect the environment. Think of some things you can do in your community to help the environment. Prepare a short speech explaining your ideas. Then give your speech to the class.

DIRECTIONS: Read the following story about a boy who has been separated from his parents. Then you will use a Story Map. It will help you write about what you think happens just after the story ends.

Smile for the Camera

by Um Yaqoob

He had beautiful features: large almond-shaped brown eyes, a delicate nose, full mouth. His hair was black, cut short. For a refugee, he was in good shape physically, though dirty and barefoot.

He stood in front of my camera and stared. "You will find my mother and father," he ordered.

I looked at him through the lens. "I hope so." I focused the lens on his face. "Smile."

"Promise," he said.

"I can't promise."

"Then I can't smile."

I snapped the photo of the boy and wrote down his vital statistics. Maiga Fofana, age 10. His parents' names. His village.

"Bye," I said when I had finished. He walked away silently.

Until sundown, I shot pictures of hundreds of children. We would post their pictures wherever we could in the war-ravaged country, hoping someone would recognize a little face and come to the camp to claim the child.

The next morning Maiga was first in line.

"Did you find my parents?" he asked.

"No," I said. "I just took your picture yesterday. I haven't even developed it yet."

"Take another."

I loaded my camera. "One photo is enough," I said. "We'll make copies and post them all over."

"You will have enough?"

"More than enough," I said.

"You are sure?"

"I'm sure."

He tilted his head. "Bye," he said, and walked away.

He was there again on the third day.

"Maiga," I said, "I don't need to take another picture of you."

"Maybe I look different now."

"No," I said, "you look pretty much the same."

"My parents will be looking for me."

"I'm sure they are looking right now."

"Then you need to take another picture," he said.

I put the camera in my lap. "I don't have enough film. I can't take two pictures of everyone!"

"Just do it for me, then."

"What about the others?" I asked. "They'll want me to do the same."

He drew close to me. I could see flecks of green in his eyes. "We won't tell them," he whispered. He winked.

I shook my head. "Sorry."

He stared at me. "Bye," he said.

"Bye."

I didn't see Maiga for several days. I was busy taking pictures and developing them for aid workers to post at other camps.

One day hundreds of people came to our camp. They held photos in their hands and hope in their wide, dark eyes. They strained their necks to see through the crowds. They called out names.

All the workers gathered to watch as adults and children ran to each other, crying and embracing. I saw family after family brought together, and I felt wonderful.

Then I saw Maiga.

He stood at the edge of the group, watching. Tears poured from his eyes. His mouth was parted in a silent cry.

I went to him, and he fell against me and sobbed into my chest. "They'll come," I said. "It's just the first day."

"They must miss me."

"I know they do," I said. "And you must miss them."

He pulled away and looked at me. "Of course I do! They're my parents, and I'm just a little boy."

I hugged him again. He melted against me. It must have been months since someone had held him. I let him hold on until he was ready to let go.

The next day, he was at the front of the line again.

"I want to help you," he said.

"It's OK," I said. "I'm doing all right."

"I can write the names."

I hesitated.

"Please," he said.

I sighed. "OK. But promise to do a good job."

He almost smiled as he took his place next to me.

Maiga had beautiful handwriting, square and even. He spoke to each child with authority as he wrote down the information. As each child left, Maiga said, "Bye."

He helped me for two months. He learned how to operate the camera and even took a few photos. He was usually quiet and withdrawn. Sometimes, though, he was animated, almost happy, and he talked about his family, his village, his school.

One day, no adults at all came to the camp. No one smiled that evening. Maiga sat next to me as I ate dinner. He started to cry.

"Maybe that's all of them," he said.

"No, there'll be more," I said. "They'll come, Maiga."

I hardly slept that night.

The next day, an aid worker came to me, smiling. Behind her was a young man. He looked just like Maiga.

"Maiga!" I could barely whisper the name.

The man sobbed, "My son is here!"

We ran together past lots of children. Maiga was leaning over a bowl of rice.

"Maiga!"

He looked up. His mouth dropped open and rice fell out. He squeaked as he stood up and fell against his father. The two sobbed together, and I stood with tears all over my cheeks.

Maiga looked up at me. "You will miss me!" he said.

"Yes, I will." I tried to stop my sobs.

"And I will miss you."

I wanted to take a picture of his smile, but no film could have captured the happiness I saw on his face.

Story Map

A **Story Map** helps you understand a story. It lists the different parts of a story in separate boxes. The Story Map below has a box for the five different parts of a story you just read about. It also has a box for the title of the story.

Read the essay question and instructions on page 55.

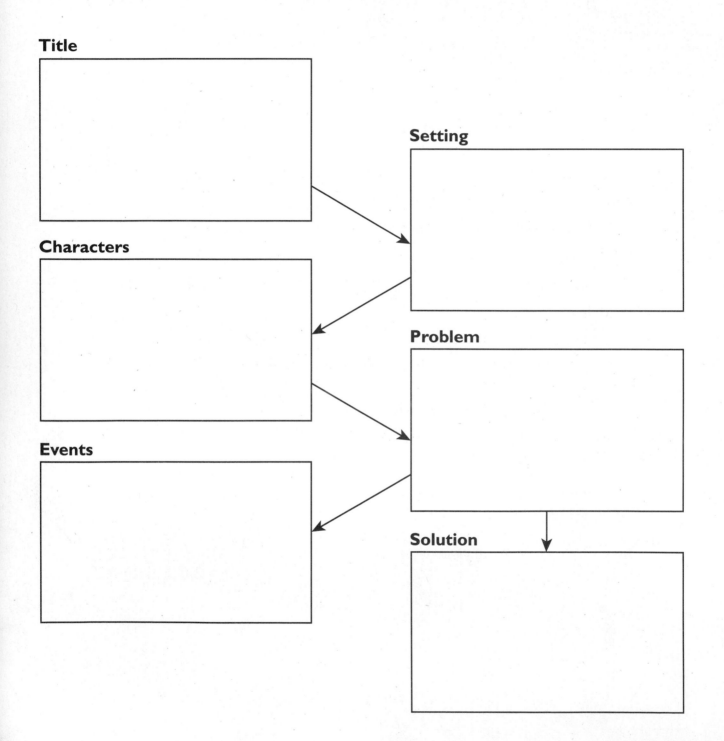

Title

Characters

Events

Setting

Problem

Solution

Essay question: What do you think happens just after the story ends? Use examples and details from the story to support your answer.

1. Start by filling in the first three boxes of the Story Map. Fill in the boxes for the Title, Setting (where and when the story takes place), and Characters.

2. For the fourth box, Problem, think about the main problem in the story. What does Maiga try to do throughout the story? What is his problem? Write this problem in the box.

3. The fifth box is the Events box. In this box, list the events in the story in the order in which they happened. Go back to the story and look for the events. List them in the box and number each one.

4. In the last box, Solution, write how Maiga's problem is solved.

Now that you have filled in the **Story Map,** use it to answer the essay question at the top of the page. Write your answer on a separate sheet of paper.

Open the Door

This question asks you to predict what will happen next in the story by listing some details about the story. This is a critical question. Look for clues just as you would if you were answering an interpretive question. Then, make a judgment—come up with your own answer based on the story and your own experiences.

Look at the Story Map you just filled in. Think about what would probably happen next in the story. What will Maiga and his father most likely do? What will the narrator do? Write at least two paragraphs telling what happens right after the story ends.

Remember to **Review**. When you are done, check your writing. Use the checklist on page 56.

After You Write

Use this list to check your writing.

Revise:
- ☐ Did you answer the question?
- ☐ Are each of your paragraphs related to the topic?
- ☐ Is there an opening and a closing?
- ☐ Did you support your main ideas with details?
- ☐ Did you organize your ideas clearly?

- ☐ Do all of your words make sense?
- ☐ Is your writing easy to read?

Edit:
- ☐ Do your verbs agree with their subjects?
- ☐ Did you use pronouns correctly?
- ☐ Are your spelling, capitalization, and punctuation correct?

Summary

In this unit, you learned how graphic organizers can help you understand what you have read. You also learned how to use graphic organizers to help you answer essay questions. A graphic organizer can help you put your thoughts in order before you begin to write.

You have learned about the following graphic organizers:

Character Traits Web

 **Venn Diagram**

 **Main Idea Map**

 **Cause and Effect Map**

 **Sequence Map**

 **Story Map**

 Remember that when answering an essay question, you should always use the **Four Rs:** Ready, Read, Respond, Review. When you review your work, use a checklist such as the one above.

Guided Practice

Now you are going to practice what you have learned by reading several selections. You will be asked to answer multiple-choice, short-answer, and essay questions about what you have read. These questions will be at the three key levels of comprehension: literal, interpretive, and critical. You will be given a hint to help you answer each question.

Regardless of what type of selection you read or question you answer, you should always follow the **Four *R*s:**

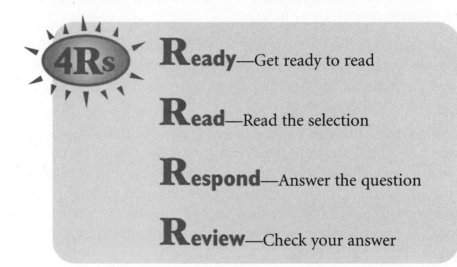

4Rs

Ready—Get ready to read

Read—Read the selection

Respond—Answer the question

Review—Check your answer

A Garden for a Roof

by Mary Houlgate

How do you build a house? Most houses are built up from the ground. Their walls are made of brick, stone, or wood. They have windows to let in light and air, doors to let in people, and a roof to keep off rain and snow. Some houses are small; some are tall apartment buildings. Look around you and you can see many different kinds of houses.

But can you imagine a house that hides underneath trees, grass, and flowers? People live in homes like this all over the world. Their houses are called "earth-sheltered" homes, and the people who build them are often called "*geotects*" (earth builders).

A geotect builds an earth-sheltered house in a shallow hole or against the side of a hill. The floor, walls, and roof are made of concrete blocks. On the sunniest side of the house are large, strong windows. The house looks quite ordinary, until the geotect hides it. Have you ever covered a friend with sand at the beach, leaving only his or her face showing? Geotects cover their houses with a deep layer of earth, leaving only the windows showing! On top of the earth, they plant grass or a garden.

Building an earth-sheltered house isn't easy. The house must have very strong walls to hold the weight of the earth that will cover it. Drains and pipes are laid around the house to suck away rain and ground water. The walls and roof must be covered with a special waterproof skin, which is melted on with a blowtorch. (One builder walked across his new roof with hobnail boots and punched dozens of holes through the waterproof skin! He had to start all over again.) If the windows don't fit their frames exactly, snails, slugs, and spiders can slip in.

Why do geotects bother? They love their homes because they're quiet, fireproof, and strong enough to last hundreds of years. Earth-sheltered houses keep the countryside green: instead of a bare roof, you see growing grass or a beautiful garden. Best of all, the houses keep the air clean. How can a building do that?

Here's how. An ordinary house is cold in winter and hot in summer. We run furnaces and air conditioners to stay comfortable, but these require the burning of coal or gas, and that can cause pollution. An earth-sheltered house is covered with a thick earthen "blanket." This means the house stays the same cool temperature inside, winter, and summer, like a cave or your basement. Summer and winter, just a little heat is needed to make an earth-sheltered house comfortable. Many earth-sheltered homes use the sun as a furnace. It warms the house when it shines through the windows. The concrete blocks in the floor and walls soak up this heat and keep the house warm all night. With no furnace and no air conditioners, the house uses very little fuel. The air stays a lot cleaner!

How did geotects think up the idea of "hiding" a house? They looked into the past. For thousands of years, people from China to North Africa to France have dug homes beneath the earth. The Anasazi, a Native American people, once lived in round pits covered over with logs and mud. Later, American pioneers like Laura Ingalls Wilder used "dugouts," homes made quickly in hollowed-out riverbanks.

What's it like to live underneath two feet of dirt? Isn't it dismal and damp? Not at all! Geotects work hard to make their houses bright and airy. They put fans into each room to draw in fresh air and push out stale air. The large windows are designed so that sunlight pours through them. Some poke up through the roof as glass domes or pyramids. Imagine standing on your bed, sticking your head up into your dome window, and saying hello to a rabbit nibbling the grass on your roof! Earth-sheltered homes sometimes have indoor gardens, even indoor swimming pools.

Geotects want to help the environment by building more than just houses. They are helping to hide office buildings, museums, ice rinks, and libraries under earth blankets. These large buildings use only a little fuel. And instead of a roof, they have a garden!

1 *Geotects* are people who—

   A build houses up from the ground

   B live in tall apartment buildings

   C build houses in the earth

   D earn a living studying the earth

 Hint This is a vocabulary question. The answer is right in the article. Go back to the beginning of the article and find the word *geotect*.

2 What would be another good title for this article?

   F "How to Build a House"

   G "Helping the Environment"

   H "Hidden Houses"

   J "The History of Dugouts"

Hint Figure out the main idea of the article. What is the article mostly about? Determining the main idea will help you choose a good title.

3 Which of these is an *opinion* from the article?

   A Building an earth-sheltered house isn't easy.

   B Many earth-sheltered homes use the sun as a furnace.

   C The floor, walls, and roof are made of concrete blocks.

   D The large windows allow sunlight into the home.

 Hint Identify an opinion from the article. An *opinion* is what someone **believes** to be true. A *fact* is something that **is** true.

Answers

1 Ⓐ Ⓑ Ⓒ Ⓓ	2 Ⓕ Ⓖ Ⓗ Ⓙ	3 Ⓐ Ⓑ Ⓒ Ⓓ

Guided Practice   **Unit 3**

4 How do earth-sheltered homes help keep the air clean?

_____

_____

_____

_____

_____

_____

 Hint Identify details from the article. Skim the article to find the paragraph that discusses how earth-sheltered homes keep the air clean.

5 Would you like to live in an earth-sheltered home? Why or why not?

_____

_____

_____

_____

_____

_____

Hint Draw a conclusion based on what you read. Go back to the article and find reasons to support your conclusion.

6 Compare and contrast a regular house with an earth-sheltered house. Use information from the article along with your own observations.

Use a graphic organizer to plan your essay.

 A Venn Diagram will help you organize your thoughts about the houses. Draw a Venn Diagram in the space below. List what is different about each house in the outside ovals. Write what is the same about the houses in the center where the ovals overlap.

Write your essay on the lines below. If you need more space, continue writing on a separate sheet of paper.

_____

_____

_____

_____

_____

_____

_____

_____

_____

_____

_____

_____

 Hint Here you must compare and contrast, using details from the article. Look at the information you wrote in the Venn Diagram. You might want to begin your essay by telling how the two houses are different. Then, in a second paragraph, explain how they are alike. After you finish, use the checklist on page 56 to help you review your writing.

This page may not be reproduced without permission of Steck-Vaughn/Berrent.

DIRECTIONS: The Kumeyaay Indians live in southern California. Read this Kumeyaay folktale about a bold rabbit. Then answer questions 7 through 12. Darken the circle at the bottom of the page or write your answer on the lines.

Running Rabbit
A Kumeyaay Folktale

retold by Jeannie Beck

There was once a rabbit who was known to be the fastest rabbit in the world. The elders often spoke of this rabbit whenever a young boy came of age and it was time to test his hunting skills.

One small boy, who had heard the tale of this rabbit many times, decided that he would be the one to finally bring him in. As the years passed and the boy came of age, still no one had managed to bag Running Rabbit.

The elders cheered the boy on as he carved his first bow and arrow. He was given three days to hunt the rabbit. It was known that this rabbit always stayed in a certain flat area that was at least a mile long. It was here that the boy waited until he saw Running Rabbit.

"I have waited for you for a long time, and now you are old and it is time for you to leave this world," the boy said to the rabbit as he drew back his arrow. But by the time the arrow had left the bow, the rabbit had disappeared.

"That rabbit doesn't seem to get older, he just gets faster," the boy said to himself.

As night fell, the boy returned to camp, hearing the elders cheering his arrival because they had thought for sure that he would be the one to bring in the tricky old rabbit.

The boy did not hunt the next day, but instead searched for the strongest, straightest greasewood plant. From this plant he formed the *sleekest* arrow.

Then he found the healthiest, most powerful elderberry tree from which he carved his new bow.

The boy decorated his new tool with elegant feathers from the magical flicker bird. Finally he shaped the sharpest, longest arrowhead, creating the least amount of wind resistance. When all was prepared, he fell asleep satisfied.

The next morning the boy returned to the flat and waited with complete confidence for Running Rabbit. As he strained his eyes to see through the early morning mist, he spied a streak of dust cutting through the fog. There he was!

The boy drew back his bow, and as the arrow left, so did the rabbit, who was showing off his fast running. About a mile away, the boy could see a large dark cloud rising up from the meadow.

When he reached the end of the flat, the boy saw a strange thing. There was his arrow, with the flicker feathers flying in the breeze, pinning a rabbit's fur to the ground. But where was Running Rabbit? The boy searched the meadow for hours before finally returning to camp with just the rabbit's soft coat. The elders thought the boy had made rabbit stew before returning home, so no one ever asked.

But the truth was, instead of running away from the boy, the rabbit had been showing off, and when he jumped so high and fast he ran into the arrow's path and got skinned. Running Rabbit narrowly escaped with his life, but not before losing his beautiful coat.

The naked rabbit was so embarrassed that he had to hide until he grew a new coat, and from then on he was shy like all the other rabbits.

7 Another word for *sleekest* is—

F smallest   H roundest

G smoothest   J dullest

 Hint This is a vocabulary question. You can figure out the meaning of the word from the sentence before this one in the story.

8 The boxes show some things that happened in the story.

The boy makes a bow and arrow from a greasewood plant and an elderberry tree.		The rabbit's fur is pinned to the ground by the boy's arrow.
1	2	3

Which event belongs in Box 2?

A The rabbit hides until he grows a new coat.

B The elders cheer as the boy carves his first bow and arrow.

C The boy returns to the flat and waits for Running Rabbit.

D The boy is given three days to hunt Running Rabbit.

Hint What is the order of events in the story? Find each event. Which event happened *after* the event in Box 1 and *before* the event in Box 3?

9 Which of the following tells you that this story could *not* have really happened?

F A rabbit does not run fast.

G A boy could not make a bow and arrow.

H A rabbit does not live in a flat area.

J A rabbit could not be skinned by an arrow.

Hint Identify what is real and what is not real in the story. Which choice gives a reason why this story could not be true?

Answers

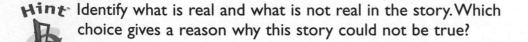

7 Ⓕ Ⓖ Ⓗ Ⓙ	8 Ⓐ Ⓑ Ⓒ Ⓓ	9 Ⓕ Ⓖ Ⓗ Ⓙ

10 Why don't the elders ask the boy what happened to the rabbit when he returns to camp with just its fur?

_____

_____

_____

_____

_____

_____

 Hint Identify details from the story. Look for the scene where the boy's arrow pins the rabbit's fur to the ground. What happens after this?

11 What lesson does the rabbit learn from losing his fur?

_____

_____

_____

_____

_____

 Hint Draw a conclusion. What does the rabbit do wrong? How does he act after he loses his fur?

12 What makes the boy such a good match for the rabbit? Use examples and details from the story to support your essay.

Use a graphic organizer to plan your essay.

 Before you can answer this, you must list some character traits about the boy that make him a good hunter. Draw a Character Traits Web in the space below. Fill in information about the boy.

Write your essay on the lines below. If you need more space, continue writing on a separate sheet of paper.

_____

_____

_____

_____

_____

_____

_____

_____

_____

_____

_____

_____

_____

 Hint   You must explain in what way the boy is a good match for the rabbit. Look at the traits you wrote in the Character Traits Web. Which ones help the boy outsmart the rabbit? Use those traits and examples to write your essay. After you finish, remember to use the checklist on page 56 to help you review your writing.

DIRECTIONS: Read this article about a man who knows all about alligators. Then answer questions 13 through 18. Darken the circle at the bottom of the page or write your answer on the lines.

Alligators Are Really Shy

by Pringle Pipkin

Imagine finding an alligator hiding under your family's car. What would you do? If you lived in South Carolina, you might call Walt Rhodes, the state's alligator expert. Mr. Rhodes has captured alligators in people's garages, toolboxes, rosebushes, and even swimming pools.

"You have to think about exactly what you're doing whenever you're handling alligators," Mr. Rhodes says.

His main job as a wildlife biologist is to study and protect alligators. For seven years, he has kept records of their births and survival. He wants to see how changes in the weather and the environment are affecting them. "That will help give us answers for management of the alligator to help it survive better in the future," he says.

These large, usually muddy reptiles have been around for millions of years. But now they need Mr. Rhodes and other scientists to help them survive in a changing world. Alligators have been losing much of their habitat as people build houses, golf courses, and shopping centers near their watery homes.

Alligators live in freshwater swamps, rivers, and marshes along the coasts of warm states such as South Carolina, Georgia, Florida, and Louisiana. In the summer, the females build large grassy nests that can hold more than forty-five eggs. Mr. Rhodes uses helicopters and boats to find nests hidden in the marsh.

Sea turtles and many kinds of snakes lay eggs and leave them to hatch on their own. But a mother alligator often floats in the water near her nest. She will pop out to protect her eggs from raccoons, bears, or other hungry animals.

Surprisingly, mother alligators do not confront Mr. Rhodes very often, even when he is digging for their eggs. He sometimes faces a female lurking near the nest or hissing and flashing her teeth. These mothers are trying to scare him away, not attack him. "But you want to keep up your guard because you never know," he says.

That's why Mr. Rhodes always takes a partner along when hunting for nests. One time, he was digging eggs out of a nest in tall grass when the mother came up from behind. His helper shouted a warning. "I bopped her on the nose with the boat paddle, and she jumped in the water," he says.

On a later visit, the same mother refused to back down. Mr. Rhodes kept swatting at her with the paddle while his partner emptied the nest.

Once he has the eggs, Mr. Rhodes hatches the baby-alligator families which are called *clutches*, in special boxes in his backyard. Hatching baby alligators gives him a way to study them at this precarious time in their lives. Mr. Rhodes always returns each baby to its mother's nest.

As young alligators grow and leave their mothers, they wander away from their homes, looking for food, a mate, or a new place to live. Usually they travel at night. If an alligator is far from the marsh when the sun comes up, it will look for someplace cool and dark to hide, such as under a car. In warmer months, when alligators are busy roaming, Mr. Rhodes is busing rounding them up.

"They are very shy animals, and that's what most people don't realize," Mr. Rhodes says. "The animals view us as a threat. We tower over them."

Some alligators don't slink away. Those that venture into places such as boat landings or golf courses can lose their fear of humans. Too often, people feed the alligators. Expecting food, some of these reptiles have approached people and attacked them. Alligators found in developed areas are often destroyed to protect people.

Once, a big alligator swam into a water pipe and ended up behind a drainage grate at a large store's parking lot. People saw the alligator and called Mr. Rhodes. The alligator was about nine feet down in the pipe.

"I laid down and crawled into the drain up to my belly," Mr. Rhodes says. "Someone held my ankles, and I was kind of bent over in the hole."

Using a long pole, Mr. Rhodes slipped a wire noose, or *snare*, over the alligator's head and tightened the wire around the reptile's neck. He eased the alligator up into the parking lot. Then he slipped a second snare over its snout and let the animal tire itself out by struggling.

While Mr. Rhode's helpers held the snares in place, he snuck up behind the alligator and squeezed its mouth shut with his hand. Then he snapped a thick rubber band over its snout, lifted the muzzled creature into the bed of his pickup truck, and hauled it away.

"Science is not all lab coats and microscopes," Mr. Rhodes says. "Some of us do get to go out and play and get muddy."

13 A mother alligator is different from sea turtles and many kinds of snakes because she—

A protects her eggs

B leaves her eggs

C sits on her eggs

D hides her eggs

 Hint Identify details. Look for the key word *eggs* in the article. How does a mother alligator care for her eggs?

14 Mr. Rhodes sometimes finds alligators near people's homes because the alligators—

F like to be around people

G have nowhere else to go

H want to scare people away

J are looking for their eggs

 Hint This is a cause and effect question. Reread the beginning of the article. What is happening to the alligators?

15 You can conclude from the article that Mr. Rhodes—

A is proud of his work

B also helps other animals

C keeps alligators as pets

D usually works at night

 Hint Here you must evaluate the article. Think about all the information the author presents about Walt Rhodes.

Answers

13 Ⓐ Ⓑ Ⓒ Ⓓ	14 Ⓕ Ⓖ Ⓗ Ⓙ	15 Ⓐ Ⓑ Ⓒ Ⓓ

16 Why does Walt Rhodes take a partner with him when he hunts for alligator nests?

_____

_____

_____

_____

_____

 Hint This question asks you to identify details. Look for key words in the article such as *nest*. Why does Mr. Rhodes need a partner?

17 What do you think Walt Rhodes does with the alligators he captures?

_____

_____

_____

_____

Hint Make a prediction. Determining what type of person Mr. Rhodes is will help you answer this question. What does he do with the baby alligators once they hatch from their eggs?

18 A job description lists the title of a job and the responsibilities related to the job. It tells what a person with the job does. Write a job description for Walt Rhodes's job. Use details from the article.

Use a graphic organizer to plan your job description.

 Draw a Main Idea Map to organize your thoughts. Put the job title at the top of the Main Idea Map. Then, include some responsibilities in the subtopic boxes. Finally, add details about each responsibility.

Write your job description on the lines below. If you need more space, continue writing on a separate sheet of paper.

_____

_____

_____

_____

_____

_____

_____

_____

_____

_____

_____

_____

Hint This question asks you to describe the main idea of the article, using supporting details. Use the information on the Main Idea Map to write your job description. Write a paragraph for each subtopic. Remember to use the checklist on page 56 to review your writing.

Speak Out

You have read how Walt Rhodes does his job as a wildlife biologist. Would you want to be a wildlife biologist? Prepare a short speech explaining why you would or would not like Walt Rhodes's job. Then give your speech to the class.

DIRECTIONS: Read this poem about a child who is enchanted by the moon. Then answer questions 19 through 24. Darken the circle at the bottom of the page or write your answer on the lines.

The New Moon
by Eliza Lee Follen

Dear mother, how pretty

The moon looks tonight!

She was never so cunning before;

Her two little horns

Are so sharp and bright,

I hope she'll not grow any more.

If I were up there,

With you and my friends,

I'd rock in it nicely, you'd see;

I'd sit in the middle

And hold by both ends.

Oh, what a bright cradle 't would be!

I would call to the stars

To keep out of the way,

Lest we should rock over their toes;

And then I would rock

Till the dawn of the day,

And see where the pretty moon goes.

And there we would stay

In the beautiful skies,

All through the bright clouds we would roam;

We would see the sun set,

And see the sun rise,

And on the next rainbow come home.

19 The speaker of the poem thinks the moon is—

F scary

G charming

H friendly

J cunning

Hint Find details from the poem. Reread the beginning of the poem. How does the speaker describe the moon?

20 When the author says the moon would be a "bright cradle," she means the moon—

A is about the size of a cradle

B shines as bright as a cradle

C is shaped like a cradle

D rocks just like a cradle

Hint This question is about vocabulary and what words mean. When the author says the moon would be a bright cradle, she is using a metaphor. Read the entire stanza to see what she is comparing in this metaphor.

21 The author probably wrote this poem to—

F tell a story about the moon

G describe what it's like to be on the moon

H tell how the moon looks to a child

J convince people to look at the moon at night

Hint Here is a question about the author's purpose. Reread the poem. What is the author trying to show with the poem?

Answers

19 Ⓕ Ⓖ Ⓗ Ⓙ	20 Ⓐ Ⓑ Ⓒ Ⓓ	21 Ⓕ Ⓖ Ⓗ Ⓙ

22 In the third stanza of the poem, why did the speaker say she would call
to the stars to keep out of the way?

_____

_____

_____

_____

_____

_____

 Hint Identify details from the poem. Reread the third stanza. What
does the speaker say after she calls to the stars to keep out of
her way?

23 What is the mood of this poem?

_____

_____

_____

_____

 Hint This question is about the mood, or tone, of the poem.
How does the speaker feel as she is describing the moon
to her mother?

24 Write a summary of the poem.

Use a graphic organizer to plan your summary.

 Draw a Sequence Map and write down the details of the speaker's fantasy. Write an event in each box in the order in which it happened. The oval next to each box is for the details about that event.

Write your summary on the lines below. If you need more space, continue writing on a separate sheet of paper.

_____

_____

_____

_____

_____

_____

_____

_____

_____

_____

_____

_____

_____

_____

_____

_____

_____

 Hint Summarize the poem by listing the order of events. Look at the events and the details you wrote in the Sequence Map. Write a few sentences about each event. Write about the events in the order in which they happened. Remember to use the checklist on page 56 to review your writing.

DIRECTIONS: Read these two stories. The first is about Mullah Nasreddin, a legendary character who appears in many Asian folktales. He solves life's problems with a mixture of foolishness and wisdom. The second is a fable about friendship. Then answer questions 25 through 30. Darken the circle at the bottom of the page or write your answer on the lines.

The Guest

retold by Uma Krishnaswami

Mullah Nasreddin was a wise man. When he spoke, people listened. And so he chose his words and actions as carefully as kings choose their generals.

One day a rich man invited the Mullah to a feast at his house. "I would be honored, Mullah sahib," said he, "if you would grace us with your presence. Tomorrow night?"

"I will come," agreed Mullah Nasreddin, "tomorrow night."

The following night, the Mullah threw on his shabbiest and most comfortable clothes. "It is a bit chilly," he said, and added an old black coat. The edges of its sleeves were frayed. The holes in its elbows were patched with swatches torn from old flour sacks.

On his feet, Mullah Nasreddin slipped a pair of ragged sandals.

When darkness fell he arrived at the rich man's doorstep. A servant opened the door. "What do you want, old man?" the servant demanded.

"Your master has invited me to his feast," said the Mullah.

The servant peered suspiciously at him. "Wait here," he said. "I'll be back in a moment."

The servant went in. His whispers carried to the door. "An old beggarman, O my master . . . says he is your guest . . ."

The rich man came to the courtyard to take a look. Seeing the old man in his ragged clothes, he waved a hand to the servant, then went back to join his elegant guests.

The servant returned to the door. "My master does not know you," he said.

"He invited me to his feast," insisted the Mullah.

The servant laughed. "Nonsense! Invited you? A ragged old beggar? My master's friends are noblemen and kings. Be off before I take a stick to you!"

So Mullah Nasreddin went home. He changed into his finest silk garments. He wore a black woolen vest with silver trim. He put his best cap on his head and added a handsome high-collared coat. He sprinkled rose water on his face and hands. He combed his beard.

Smiling to himself, he made his way back to the rich man's house and knocked at the door.

Once again, the servant opened it. Once again, the Mullah said, "Your master has invited me to his feast."

This time the servant bowed respectfully and ushered him in.

"Welcome, welcome, Mullah sahib." And the rich man himself showed the Mullah to his special seat at the feast.

"At last, Mullah sahib," said the guests. "We have all been waiting for you."

The food arrived. "Serve Mullah Nasreddin first," said the rich man. The Mullah smiled at everyone. Then he began to get busy with his food.

But he did not eat.

"Hai hai!" cried the guests.

"Mullah sahib! What are you doing?" cried the rich man.

For Mullah Nasreddin had begun to spoon the soup over his best cap. He crumbled the bread and sprinkled the crumbs over the shoulders of his handsome high-collared coat. He took apart the shish kebab and fed it lovingly to his sleeves.

The rich man's voice trembled. "Mullah sahib, do you not like the food?"

In reply, Mullah Nasreddin dribbled the delicate yogurt and cream sauces over his fine silk garments and best black woolen vest with silver trim. Then he sat back and beamed at everyone.

There was a shocked silence. Then the rich man said, "O most respected Mullah Nasreddin, you never do anything without a reason. Has someone offended you?"

The Mullah replied, "When I arrived in rags, you turned me away. Now that I am dressed in finery, you treat me with honor. Clearly it is my clothes you are welcoming and not me. So it is only fitting that they should eat this delightful food you have prepared for them."

The rich man hung his head in shame. He said, "Mullah sahib, forgive me. I was blind. I saw only your clothes and could not recognize the wearer. I will never again judge people by how they look or by the clothes they wear." And, in truth, he never did.

The Crane, the Jay, and the Peacock

Long ago in a distant land, a crane and a jay were good friends. The two went everywhere together and enjoyed each other's company. When Crane built her nest, Jay was the first one to help. When Crane was short of food one winter, Jay sacrificed some of her meager provisions. Crane knew that if she were in need, her friend would always be there for her.

One day as Crane was flying over a new neighborhood, she spotted a peacock spreading her gorgeous tail. Crane thought, "Why, that bird is robed in gold and purple and all the colors of the rainbow. I would love to be her friend." Crane flew down to Peacock and introduced herself. A new friendship began.

With her new friend occupying much of her time, Crane had little time left for Jay. When Jay asked Crane to go with her to the pond, Crane said she was too busy running an errand for Peacock. When Jay needed someone to watch her young, Crane was off frolicking with her new friend. When Jay was sick and needed help, Crane was helping Peacock groom her magnificent tail.

Crane would do anything for Peacock just to be seen with the beautiful bird. Peacock was going on vacation soon, and Crane was sure that the grand creature would ask her to come along. When she mentioned this to Peacock, the bird laughed. "Why would I want to be seen on vacation with you? I'm robed like a queen, while you have not a bit of color on your wings. You're good enough to fetch and carry for me, but not good enough to go on vacation with me."

Heartbroken, Crane visited Jay to tell her about Peacock's cruel words. But her old friend was not sympathetic. "You deserted a true friend for one with fine feathers," she said. "Now you've learned that fine feathers don't make fine birds."

25 People respected Mullah Nasreddin because he was—

  A wise

  B rich

  C powerful

  D respectful

 Hint Identify details from the story. Why do people listen when Nasreddin speaks?

26 Which two characters make similar mistakes?

  F Nasreddin and Peacock

  G The servant and Jay

  H Nasreddin and Jay

  J The rich man and Crane

 Hint Compare the characters. Which two characters make the wrong judgments?

27 What can you conclude about the rich man in "The Guest"?

  A He is willing to change his ways.

  B He is too proud to learn a lesson.

  C He says one thing and does another.

  D He treats everyone as a friend.

Hint Evaluate the meaning of the story. Think of how the rich man responds to Nasreddin's explanation.

Answers

25 Ⓐ Ⓑ Ⓒ Ⓓ	26 Ⓕ Ⓖ Ⓗ Ⓙ	27 Ⓐ Ⓑ Ⓒ Ⓓ

28 Why does Nasreddin feed his clothes?

_____

_____

_____

_____

_____

_____

 Hint Identify details from the story. Look for the scene where the rich man asks Nasreddin if someone has offended him. What does Nasreddin say to the rich man?

29 What is the lesson to be learned from _both_ stories?

_____

_____

_____

_____

Hint Make a connection between the two stories. What are the themes? Think about what happens to the characters in both stories. What lesson do they learn?

30 Write a review of one of the stories. In your review, tell a little about the story's plot. Then explain what you liked and did not like about the story. Use details from the story to support your opinion.

Use a graphic organizer to plan your review.

 Fill in a Story Map by writing down the main parts of the story. For the Setting box, you might not be able to tell exactly when and where the story takes place. Just write whatever information about the setting you can find or infer.

Write your review on the lines below. If you need more space, continue writing on a separate sheet of paper.

_____

_____

_____

_____

_____

_____

_____

_____

_____

_____

_____

Hint Evaluate one of the stories by analyzing what happens in it. Look at the items you filled in on the Story Map. Then think about the story. What do you want to tell about the plot? What parts of the story did you like? What parts would you have liked to change? After you finish, use the checklist on page 56 to review.

Test

You will now be taking a practice test. The test includes all the skills you have reviewed in this book. Follow the directions in each section. As always, remember to use the **Four *R*s: R**eady, **R**ead, **R**espond, and **R**eview. You may look back at the reading passages as needed.

For the multiple-choice questions, work carefully and try to get as many questions right as you can. Do not spend too much time on any one question. If you are not sure of an answer, make the best choice you can and go on to the next question. You can go back and check answers later if you have time.

For the open-ended questions, plan out what you want to say before writing. Use graphic organizers to help you write your essay questions. Make sure that you respond to all parts of each question. After you finish writing, use the checklist on page 56 to help you review your work.

DIRECTIONS: **Read this story about a boy who misses his homeland.**
Then answer questions 1 through 11. Darken the circle on the separate
answer sheet or write your answer on the lines.

The Word Is . . .

by C.S. Perryess

Tasi watched Martin's gym shoes fly through the cold city air, tied together like dancers holding hands.

Martin was going to throw them again, up toward the telephone lines along the street, Tasi just knew it. He wished they would just walk home to their apartment building.

"You could lose 'em," Tasi said.

"You be quiet, boy," Martin said as he swung his shoes again.

Back home on the island, on Samoa, things were different. Nobody cared here—not even your best friend. City people acted as if they didn't even need each other.

Martin's shoes made black and white patterns, spinning in a big hoop. Tasi knew Martin's mama didn't have extra money for new gym shoes.

The shoes sailed into the air, up by the palm tree in front of the Palm Apartments, dancing away. Then they wrapped perfectly around the top of a streetlight.

"What—?" Martin said, with his eyes all big and his voice getting squeaky.

The shoes swung to a stop. Martin kicked the pole that held up the streetlight.

Tasi's mom and auntie wouldn't be home till after dark. He stood in their apartment, looking through the window at the cold streets. People pushed past one another. Cars honked.

"People here," he said to the glass in the window, "they don't get it." Back home the word was *aiga* (ah-inga). They say *aiga* means family, but that isn't all. It means making the people around you number one.

He thought about Martin and what Martin's mama would say. He remembered those shoes on the post and that one leaning palm tree.

Back home there were *niu* trees—they looked about the same as palm trees here but they grew coconuts. Everybody worked together to make houses, roofs, mats—all from parts of the *niu* tree. They even got together to eat the coconuts. Island people did everything together.

But here? All those people walking all alone, so fast, with their heads down, and that poor tree out there with no coconuts.

The sun set brown and dirty behind the big buildings. Tasi stood in his baggy shorts and bare feet, just under that palm tree. He shivered, but who could climb in jeans and shoes? He held his *lavalava* in his hands.

"*Li'o*," he whispered, twisting the fabric as if he were wringing out a dish towel.

"*Milo*," he said, tying it in a circle. It was good to hear the right words.

He looped one end of the twisted *lavalava* around each foot. It was a thick tree, so he had to hold close.

"Somebody's gotta . . ."

Inch.

" . . . do something good . . ."

Inch.

" . . . in this unfriendly place," he said on his way up.

A car stereo's deep *foom foom* blared out over the traffic noise.

Inch. Inch.

Yellow streetlights glinted off the top of a city bus. There were no stars.

Inch. Inch.

The climb got easier where the tree leaned over. The trunk was rough, but that was OK. The word is *malo*. He was doing a *good job* in a gloomy place. Would anybody else here do that?

Inch. Inch.

Just a few moves to go. Little reflector triangles on Martin's shoes glittered in the streetlights' glare.

A yell came from below. "No!" It was somebody's mama.

She flapped her arms around at the cars going by. Brakes screeched. Doors slammed.

Inch. Inch.

Two moves to go.

"Hey!" came a deep voice. "Hang tight, son." From up so high the man looked like a little head in the middle of a black hole.

"Help him!" somebody's mama called. Now there were more people, all looking up.

One move to go. All the shouting people were a long way down—a very long way down.

The head in the black hole shouted up, "Don't get scared, son!" Tasi's leg started to jiggle.

That wiggling leg would just have to cool it. Tasi gave a shove.

A dozen people below sucked in their breath.

"I can't watch!" someone said.

Tasi held tight with one hand. With the other he reached out to the closest shoe. Tug, tug. He pulled that shoe down as the other went up. Once it popped over the post, he let go and the shoes dropped.

Everybody screamed.

"Calm down." It was the Black Hole Man. "It's just his shoes."

Slide, push, slide. Tasi headed down.

"Careful!"

"Oh, man!"

His feet touched the ground.

"Praise the Lord."

Somebody's mama wrapped fleshy arms around him and started crying. She smelled like vanilla.

She let go and a circle of people were looking right at him. Two of them were wiping their eyes.

"Let's get you home, son." That was the Black Hole Man. He was as big as Uncle Seni, but wearing a suit. He handed over Martin's shoes.

Then the Black Hole Man put his big hand on Tasi's shoulder, and the whole bunch of them walked him all the way home. Cars and buses roared and honked, and there weren't any stars. Still, as Tasi told them about Martin's shoes and *aiga*, they all listened. They kept walking with him. Maybe this city wasn't so gloomy after all.

When they reached his apartment building, Tasi looked up at them all.

"The word is *malo*," he said. "It means *good job* and *thanks*, all at once."

The Black Hole Man nodded his head, "Well, son," he said, looking at the shoes slung over Tasi's shoulder. "*Malo*."

1 In the first paragraph, the phrase "tied together like dancers holding hands" is an example of—

   A personification

   B hyperbole

   C a metaphor

   D a simile

2 What is a *lavalava*?

   F A cloth used for climbing

   G A type of tree in Samoa

   H A person who helps others

   J A towel for washing

3 Which is an *opinion* from the story?

   A Martin kicked the pole that held up the streetlight.

   B Tasi knew Martin's mama didn't have extra money for new gym shoes.

   C City people acted as if they didn't even need each other.

   D He was as big as Uncle Seni, but wearing a suit.

4 What would be another good title for this story?

   F "Martin's Shoes"

   G "The Black Hole Man"

   H "Climbing a Tree"

   J "Not So Gloomy After All"

5 Which of these words *best* describes Tasi?

    A shy

    B homesick

    C content

    D selfish

6 What is the *main* problem in the story?

    F Tasi is angry with Martin.

    G Tasi does not like his new home.

    H Tasi is afraid to climb a tree.

    J Tasi wishes the palm trees had coconuts.

7 The boxes show some things that happened in the story.

Martin's gym shoes wrap around a streetlight.		Tasi sees the Black Hole Man.
1	2	3

Which event belongs in Box 2?

    A The people walk Tasi home.

    B Tasi climbs a tall tree.

    C A woman gives Tasi a big hug.

    D Tasi tells the people what *malo* means.

8 From the story you can conclude that—

    F Tasi will go back to Samoa

    G Tasi will no longer talk to Martin

    H Tasi will teach his friends to climb trees

    J Tasi will be happier in his new home

9 How is Samoa different from Tasi's new home?

_____

_____

_____

_____

_____

_____

_____

10 Why does Tasi try to get Martin's shoes? Give two reasons and explain your answer.

_____

_____

_____

_____

_____

_____

_____

Write a summary of "The Word Is..." Include the most important events and details from the story in your answer.

Use a graphic organizer to plan your summary.

Write your summary on the lines below. If you need more space, continue writing on a separate sheet of paper.

_____

_____

_____

_____

_____

_____

_____

_____

_____

_____

_____

_____

_____

_____

_____

_____

_____

DIRECTIONS: Read this poem adapted from an Aesop fable. Then answer questions 12 through 22. Darken the circle on the separate answer sheet or write your answer on the lines.

The Ant and the Cricket

A silly young cricket, accustomed to sing
Through the warm, sunny months of gay summer and spring,
Began to complain when he found that, at home,
His cupboard was empty, and winter was come.
        Not a crumb to be found
        On the snow-covered ground;
        Not a flower could he see,
        Not a leaf on a tree.
"Oh! what will become," says the cricket, "of me?"

At last, by starvation and **famine** made bold,
All dripping with wet, and all trembling with cold,
Away he set off to a *miserly* ant,
To see if, to keep him alive, he would grant
        Him shelter from rain,
        And a mouthful of grain.
        He wished only to borrow;
        He'd repay it tomorrow;
If not, he must die of starvation and sorrow.

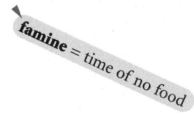

famine = time of no food

Says the ant to the cricket, "I'm your servant and friend,
But we ants never borrow; we ants never lend.
But tell me, dear cricket, did you lay nothing by
When the weather was warm?" **Quoth** the cricket, "Not I!
        My heart was so light
        That I sang day and night,
        For all nature looked **gay**."
        "You sang, sir, you say?
Go, then," says the ant, "and dance winter away!"

quoth = said

gay = happy

12 What did the cricket do in the spring and summer?

   A He danced and sang.

   B He stored food.

   C He built a warm shelter.

   D He read and told stories.

13 Which word *best* describes the cricket?

   F angry

   G foolish

   H friendly

   J wise

14 The ant probably thinks the cricket—

   A will find some food on his own

   B is getting what he deserves

   C will find someone else to help him

   D has had some very bad luck

15 Which words *best* describe the ant?

   F Shy and unsure

   G Selfish and mean

   H Friendly and helpful

   J Carefree and happy

16 The ant has food because he—

    A has a beautiful singing voice

    B stays away from crickets

    C has a warm place to live

    D worked hard during the summer

17 What is the theme of the poem?

    F Good friends are hard to find.

    G Treat others as you want to be treated.

    H Plan for the future.

    J Never borrow or lend.

18 What does the word *miserly* mean in the poem?

    A kindly

    B not young

    C quick

    D not generous

19 The author probably wrote this poem to—

    F show how ants and crickets are different

    G persuade readers to help others

    H describe how ants live in the winter

    J teach a lesson about hard work

20 How is the cricket different from the ant?

_____

_____

_____

_____

_____

_____

_____

21 What do you think happens to the cricket after the poem ends?

_____

_____

_____

_____

_____

_____

_____

22 Do you agree with the way the ant treated the cricket? Why or why not? In your answer, use information from the selection and your own ideas.

Use a graphic organizer to plan your essay.

Write your essay on the lines below. If you need more space, continue writing on a separate sheet of paper.

_____

_____

_____

_____

_____

_____

_____

_____

_____

_____

_____

_____

_____

_____

_____

_____

DIRECTIONS: Read this article about why people yawn. Then answer questions 23 through 33. Darken the circle on the separate answer sheet or write your answer on the lines.

YAAAAAAWNING

by Haleh V. Samiei

This article is going to cast a spell on you. As you read it, pressure will build behind your eardrums, and you'll lift your eyebrows and open your mouth wide. You'll hold this position for about six seconds as you take in a deep breath and then let a shorter one out.

Don't panic. It's just a contagious yawn. When you read about yawning, see someone yawning, or just think about yawning, you usually yawn yourself. But what's the purpose of yawning? Most people think that the answer is simple. You yawn when you're bored or sleepy. Some people think you yawn because you need extra oxygen. Is it true?

Robert Provine, a scientist at the University of Maryland-Baltimore County, set out to find out. The first thing he did was to test whether people yawn when they're bored. Provine had no problem boring an unlucky group of people by making them watch a video of color-bar patterns. A different, lucky group got to watch a music video. No need to say that the people in the first group won the yawning contest.

To see if people yawn more when they're sleepy, Provine had his students keep a yawn diary for a week. Whenever they yawned, they had to write down the time. As you might guess, they yawned at night when they were tired and sleepy. But Provine also found that they yawned when they woke up in the morning.

When he thought about it, he realized that when people stretch, there's a good chance they'll also yawn. In fact, other scientists have also noticed that yawning and stretching are linked. For example, the muscles of people paralyzed on one side of their body jerk as they yawn, even though they can't make the muscles move on purpose.

People also yawn when they can't possibly be bored or sleepy. Skydivers yawn just as they're about to jump out of an airplane. Concert violinists yawn just before going on stage. Olympic athletes yawn just before a big competition. Provine thinks these people may be yawning because they're nervous. He thinks that when you're nervous, sleepy, bored, or have just awakened, yawning can help focus your attention.

Ronald Baenninger, a scientist at Temple University, agrees with Provine. He and his wife Mary Anne, a scientist at The College of New Jersey, guessed that yawning helps you stay awake or become excited. They tested their guess by hooking up people to machines that measured changes in their bodies as they yawned. They found that as people yawned, they moved their wrists more than usual, they began sweating, and their hearts beat faster. This shows that these people were trying to stay awake, not fall asleep.

So what does yawning do that helps keep you alert? Provine thinks that by yawning, you stretch the muscles in your face and bring more blood to the brain. "It stirs things up," he says. The brain can then wake up the body through the fidgeting, sweating, and the faster heartbeat. You can see how this might help you stay awake at night, wake up in the morning, or become alert when you're bored or nervous.

Provine also tested whether people yawn to breathe in more oxygen. He had people breathe in a special mix of air that had less oxygen than usual. To get the oxygen they needed, people had to breathe faster. "We had people huffing and puffing," he says. "But they didn't yawn any more than they did before."

He didn't stop there. He also made people breathe in air that was *all* oxygen. They had more than enough oxygen in their blood, but they yawned as much as before. So the idea that we yawn to get more oxygen can't be right.

But not everyone agrees with Provine and the Baenningers. Some scientists think that yawning has no purpose. They say that it's a habit left over from when you were developing as a baby in your mother's womb or one you inherited from our animal ancestors. Yawning might help get the face and jaw muscles of unborn babies working, and it might help animals stay alert.

It's amazing how difficult it is get to the bottom of something as simple as a yawn.

23 Another word for *contagious* is—

A simple

B small

C helpful

D catching

24 The people watching a video of color-bar patterns yawned because they were—

F sleepy

G bored

H scared

J awake

25 Provine thinks that skydivers yawn before they jump out of an airplane because they are—

A tired

B nervous

C bored

D angry

26 Baenninger thinks that yawning helps you—

F fall asleep

G lift your eyebrows

H stay awake

J move your legs

27 Why did Provine have his students keep a yawn diary?

    A To see when they yawned

    B To see who yawned the most

    C To see how many times a week they yawned

    D To see where they were when they yawned

28 Which is an *opinion* from the article?

    F Provine found that people yawn when they wake up in the morning.

    G Sometimes athletes yawn before a big game.

    H Provine thinks you stretch the muscles in your face to bring blood to your brain.

    J It's amazing how difficult it is to get to the bottom of something as simple as a yawn.

29 Provine thinks that when we breathe in more oxygen we—

    A yawn more than before

    B yawn about the same as before

    C yawn less than before

    D yawn bigger than before

30 In the future, scientists will probably—

    F try to learn more about yawning

    G see why some people are more nervous than others

    H study animals that yawn instead of people

    J stop studying yawning

31 Why is yawning difficult for scientists to explain?

_____

_____

_____

_____

_____

_____

_____

32 Why do you think the author wrote this article?

_____

_____

_____

_____

_____

_____

_____

33 When do you yawn most often? Do you agree with Provine's findings? Why or why not? Use details from the article to support your answer.

Use a graphic organizer to plan your essay.

Write your essay on the lines below. If you need more space, continue writing on a separate sheet of paper.

_____

_____

_____

_____

_____

_____

_____

_____

_____

_____

_____

_____

_____

_____

_____

_____

Citizen Carmen

by Fabiola Santiago

Carmen walked up to the silver water fountain in the hallway, her hands damp and her mouth as dry as an empty well. A new school day stretched before her, and Carmen had butterflies in her stomach again. Maybe a cool sip of water would help.

She tucked her curls behind her ears and bent to reach the chilly trickle when, out of the corner of her eye, Carmen saw an older girl walking her way. The girl wore a bright orange belt with a silver patch that said School Patrol.

"What are you doing in the hall?" the patrol girl scolded Carmen. "The late bell is about to ring!"

Carmen searched her brain for the right words in English. She wanted to explain that she had permission from Mrs. Smith to get a drink of water. But she knew that even if the words came to her lips, she could not make them sound as crisp as the American girl's. This fear left her speechless. It was as if all her smart brain cells went to sleep every time she walked into her new school in the United States.

"I don't speak good English. I'm a Cuban girl," Carmen said slowly.

The girl stared at Carmen as if she were wondering how anyone could go to this school and not speak English.

"You're going to be in trouble if you don't get to class on time," the girl said, pointing her index finger at Carmen.

Carmen dreamed of the day that she would open her mouth and the English words would flow in beautiful, musical tones. But every day in school she was reminded that she did not speak English well. Most of all, she *dreaded* reading out loud in class.

"Carmen, please read from the board," Mrs. Smith had asked yesterday.

Carmen started to sweat, bite her lip, tap her foot.

"Sh-shair, sh-shicken," she read, squeezing her eyes shut from the effort.

"Ch-cheet, ch-cheet of paper," she heard herself say.

Her classmates broke out in giggles. Even the other Cuban students laughed. They had been in the United States longer and spoke better English.

Carmen always practiced at home, but when she had to speak in public, she became so nervous she couldn't get those *sh* and *ch* sounds right. It was embarrassing being the only fourth-grader who was afraid to read from Mrs. Smith's blackboard.

Oh, how Carmen wanted to go home to Cuba, her alligator shaped island in the Caribbean Sea. She missed her old school, her friends, her teachers, and the soulful sound of Spanish, her parents' language. In Cuba no one laughed at her because Carmen was the smartest girl in class.

Even her English had been good there! Señor Lopez, who had lived for a long time in the United States, gave Carmen English lessons every day. He thought Carmen would make a fine American. He told her so.

"Carmen, you will love the Unites States," Señor Lopez had said. "You're almost an American, you speak English so well."

But now that Carmen was in America, her English didn't sound so good. She didn't want to go back to Mrs. Smith's class. She wanted to close her eyes and wake up in Spanish at home!

R-i-i-i-n-g! The bell interrupted Carmen's daydream.

The first notes to the song Carmen liked so much crackled over the loudspeakers, and the patrol girl hurried off. Whenever Carmen heard this song at the start of the school day, she forgot about her accent. Even if she didn't know the words, she could enjoy the melody of the violins and hum along.

With the sound of the late bell, Carmen remembered that the school day was about to begin, and she hurried to her classroom. But Mrs. Smith stopped Carmen when she rushed into the room.

"You must stand in respect whenever you hear this song," Mrs. Smith whispered, bending down to reach her ear. "It's the national anthem of the United States."

Carmen stood tall at attention. After the song had ended, she told Mrs. Smith how much she liked it.

"Will you teach me the words?" Carmen asked. Although she didn't realize it, Carmen said this in pretty good English.

Mrs. Smith smiled sweetly, the way Carmen's favorite teacher did in Cuba.

"Of course," Mrs. Smith said. "I would be happy to teach you 'The Star-Spangled Banner.'"

Right away, she gave Carmen the first line to learn.

"'Oh, say, can you see,'" Mrs. Smith said slowly. "Repeat after me. 'Oh, say, can you see.'"

Carmen spent all day saying the words until she knew them by heart. Mrs. Smith was so impressed with her effort that she asked Carmen to stay after school. Day after day, she taught her a new stanza until Carmen had learned the entire song.

Mrs. Smith said that Carmen had other talents: a crisp alto voice and a good ear to catch the melody. "How would you like to join our school chorus, the Stars and Stripes?" she asked.

At first, Carmen was a little scared to sing—in English!—in front of everyone. But she felt lucky to have been picked to sing her favorite American song with the chorus.

Carmen especially liked the last line: "The land of the free and the home of the brave."

Freedom. That's why Carmen's family had come to live in the United States, her father always said.

Now that she understood the words, whenever she sang "The Star-Spangled Banner," Carmen felt proud of becoming an American.

"Carmen Gonzalez," said Mrs. Smith after Carmen's first performance with the Stars and Stripes. "What a fine American citizen you will make!"

34 In the first paragraph, the phrase "as dry as an empty well" is an example of—

A   a hyperbole

B   a simile

C   a metaphor

D   personification

35 Why does Carmen have trouble talking to the School Patrol girl?

F   She is afraid of the girl.

G   She is just learning to speak English.

H   She is nervous because she is late for class.

J   The other children in the hall are very loud.

36 How are Señor Lopez, Carmen's English teacher in Cuba, and Mrs. Smith alike?

A   They live in Cuba.

B   They teach fourth grade.

C   They are friends of Carmen's family.

D   They believe in Carmen.

37 What is Carmen's *main* problem?

F   The late bell is about to ring.

G   Her classmates have laughed at her.

H   Her English is difficult to understand.

J   She wants to go home to Cuba.

38 Carmen's family moved to the United States because they wanted—

   A to be free

   B to get better jobs

   C to go to school

   D to make new friends

39 You can tell that *dreaded* means—

   F looked forward to

   G could not understand

   H did not like

   J was in need of

40 Learning the words to "The Star-Spangled Banner" helped Carmen to—

   A get to know her classmates

   B become a better singer

   C remember her friends in Cuba

   D learn to speak English

41 Which of these sentences would fit *best* at the end of this story?

   F Carmen knew her fear would some day return.

   G Mrs. Smith became one of Carmen's favorite people.

   H For the first time, Carmen believed that she did belong in her new country.

   J Carmen thought that she would like to be a singer one day.

42 What does Carmen miss about Cuba?

_____

_____

_____

_____

_____

_____

_____

43 What do you think is the theme of this story?

_____

_____

_____

_____

_____

_____

_____

44 A character sketch is a description of someone's personality. It includes details and examples to explain what he or she is like. Write a character sketch of Carmen.

Use a graphic organizer to plan your character sketch.

Write your character sketch on the lines below. If you need more space, continue writing on a separate sheet of paper.

_____

_____

_____

_____

_____

_____

_____

_____

_____

_____

_____

_____

_____

_____

Directions: First read the article about a young Egyptian king. Next read the notice about a museum exhibit. Then answer questions 45 through 55. Darken the circle on the separate answer sheet or write your answer on the lines.

The Boy King

by Andrea Ross

How would you like to wake up one morning and be told that you are the ruler of your country? That is what happened over three thousand years ago to an Egyptian boy who was about nine years old.

Around 1370 B.C. a boy was born in a royal palace in Egypt. His name was Tutankhaten, which means "the living image of the sun god." He lived in a town in Egypt named El-Amarna during his early childhood, probably in the same palace as the **pharaoh,** Akhenaten, and his wife, Queen Nefertiti. Most historians think Tutankhaten and Akhenaten were brothers, though no one knows for sure.

The walls of the palace were painted in rich, bright colors. The floors were decorated with colored clay tiles, and the furniture was covered with real gold. Beautiful gardens and pools around the palace helped keep the air cool.

In ancient Egypt the average life span was short by today's standards. Every boy in line for the throne had to be trained in case the time ever came for him to become a pharaoh. Tutankhaten most likely started studying when he was about four years old. His education would have included learning **hieroglyphics** and mathematics. He would have written on **papyrus,** and if his answers were wrong, his tutor would have marked them in red ink.

pharaoh = ruler of ancient Egypt

hieroglyphics = pictures or symbols that stand for words, sounds, or ideas

papyrus = paper made from the papyrus plant that grows along the Nile River

Tutankhaten probably spent lots of time practicing sports. He would have learned to wrestle, swim, shoot a bow and arrow, and drive a two-horse charot. When he stayed indoors, he might have played a game called senet that is not unlike today's checkers.

Eventually Tutankhaten's brother Akhenaten died. Tutankhaten was next in line for the throne, and he became the new king. He was about nine years old at the time. As part of becoming the new pharaoh, Tutankhaten had to marry his seven-year-old niece, the daughter of Akhenaten. Since she was the royal heiress, their marriage gave Tutankhaten the right to the throne.

Tutankhaten ruled successfully for the next few years with his wife. When he was about thirteen, the temples of Egypt displayed an announcement that

praised all the things he had done to help the kingdom. These announcements were carved on flat pieces of stone. When he turned sixteen, Tutankhaten was considered a man and ruled the kingdom alone.

Tutankhaten was a great sportsman and seemed to like hunting particularly. Some of the objects from his tomb show him in a chariot aiming his bow at ostriches. He probably also hunted gazelles and antelopes.

It seems that Tutankhaten and his wife got along well. In a picture on the back of his throne she is shown bathing her husband in perfume. In another picture from that time she kneels at his feet and hands him arrows while pointing out a duck for him to shoot.

Eventually, Tutankhaten decided to change his name to Tutankh*amen*. Amen was the god of Thebes, the city his family was from.

When Tutankhamen was about seventeen, scholars think he somehow suffered a head injury. Perhaps he was wounded in battle, or maybe he was hurt while hunting. He might even have had enemies who were trying to kill him. We don't know for sure if this wound caused his death, but it is likely that he never recovered from it.

More than three thousand years later, an English **archaeologist** named Howard Carter found Tutankhamen's tomb. It yielded some of the most beautiful Egyptian treasures ever found and made the pharaoh's name famous all over the world. Though his rule was short-lived, Tutankhamen, "the boy king," will never be forgotten because of the riches he left behind.

archaeologist = scientist who studies the remains of ancient cultures

The Hunter Museum   # KING TUT

EXHIBIT

The Hunter Museum is proud to announce the arrival of the **King Tut Exhibit,** featuring treasures from King Tutankhamen's tomb.

The exhibit spans four rooms: Decoration, Sports and Games, Carvings, and Furnishings. Here are some samples of what you will find in each room:

Decoration

▲ A necklace representing the right eye of the Egyptian sun god
▲ A royal scepter made of wood and gold
▲ A protective charm in the shape of a vulture

Sports and Games

▲ Four senet game boards
▲ A bow and arrow used by the pharaoh
▲ A two-horse chariot with gold engravings

Carvings

▲ A carved, golden lion-head placed on one of the beds found in the tomb (with colored glass nose and eyes)
▲ A sculpture of King Tut rising above a lotus flower
▲ A funeral mask made of gold with glass eyes

Furnishings

▲ King Tut's magnificent throne
▲ King Tut's solid gold coffin
▲ A storage chest with picture of the king and his wife on top
▲ A child-sized chair made of ebony and ivory

Admission to the museum is free, but tickets to the exhibit will be $5.00 for adults and $2.50 for children under 12 and for senior citizens. Order tickets in advance by calling 555-4958. You won't want to miss this truly amazing exhibit.

March 9 through April 13

45 What would be another good title for "The Boy King"?

   A "The Life of King Tutankhamen"

   B "Training to Be Pharaoh"

   C "Life in Ancient Egypt"

   D "The Treasures of King Tutankhamen's Tomb"

46 The two passages are alike because they *both* describe—

   F life in ancient Egypt

   G King Tut's things

   H King Tut's family

   J temples in Egypt

47 The author probably wrote "The Boy King" to—

   A convince readers to go to the Hunter Museum

   B describe what it was like to be King

   C inform readers about King Tut's life

   D describe King Tut's personality

48 According to the article, Tutankhamen will never be forgotten because—

   F he ruled a long time

   G he did many good things

   H the treasures in his tomb were beautiful

   J many books were written about him

49 The boxes show some things that happened in the life of Tutankhamen.

He became the pharaoh.		He suffered a head injury.
1	2	3

Which event belongs in Box 2?

A He changed his name.

B He was trained to be King.

C He practiced sports.

D His treasures were discovered.

50 How much would a child have to pay to see the museum exhibit?

F $2.00

G $2.50

H $5.00

J $5.50

51 Suppose you wanted to see a necklace that looks like the right eye of the sun god. Which room in the museum would you visit?

A Decoration

B Sports and Games

C Carvings

D Furnishings

52 Which is an *opinion* from the selections?

F King Tut's brother had been the king.

G Howard Carter discovered King Tut's tomb.

H The display at the Howard Museum will be there until April 13.

J You won't want to miss this truly amazing exhibit.

53 Name three ways Tutankhamen spent his time as a boy.

_____

_____

_____

_____

_____

_____

54 What is an item mentioned in "The Boy King" that could appear in the museum exhibit if it had been found? In which room should it go?

_____

_____

_____

_____

_____

_____

55 Compare and contrast your life today with King Tut's life in ancient Egypt.

Use a graphic organizer to plan your essay.

Write your essay on the lines below. If you need more space, continue writing on a separate sheet of paper.

_____

_____

_____

_____

_____

_____

_____

_____

_____

_____

_____

_____

_____

_____

_____

Answer Sheet

STUDENT'S NAME

LAST	FIRST	MI

(Bubble columns for letters A–Z for each position)

SCHOOL: _____

TEACHER: _____

FEMALE ○   MALE ○

BIRTH DATE

MONTH	DAY	YEAR
Jan ○	⓪ ⓪	⑦ ⓪
Feb ○	① ①	⑧ ①
Mar ○	② ②	⑨ ②
Apr ○	③ ③	⓪ ③
May ○	④	④
Jun ○	⑤	⑤
Jul ○	⑥	⑥
Aug ○	⑦	⑦
Sep ○	⑧	⑧
Oct ○	⑨	⑨
Nov ○		
Dec ○		

GRADE ③ ④ ⑤ ⑥ ⑦ ⑧

Reading & Writing Excellence Level D

TEST

1 Ⓐ Ⓑ Ⓒ Ⓓ	11 essay	21 short-answer	31 short-answer	41 Ⓕ Ⓖ Ⓗ Ⓙ	51 Ⓐ Ⓑ Ⓒ Ⓓ
2 Ⓕ Ⓖ Ⓗ Ⓙ	12 Ⓐ Ⓑ Ⓒ Ⓓ	22 essay	32 short-answer	42 short-answer	52 Ⓕ Ⓖ Ⓗ Ⓙ
3 Ⓐ Ⓑ Ⓒ Ⓓ	13 Ⓕ Ⓖ Ⓗ Ⓙ	23 Ⓐ Ⓑ Ⓒ Ⓓ	33 essay	43 short-answer	53 short-answer
4 Ⓕ Ⓖ Ⓗ Ⓙ	14 Ⓐ Ⓑ Ⓒ Ⓓ	24 Ⓕ Ⓖ Ⓗ Ⓙ	34 Ⓐ Ⓑ Ⓒ Ⓓ	44 essay	54 short-answer
5 Ⓐ Ⓑ Ⓒ Ⓓ	15 Ⓕ Ⓖ Ⓗ Ⓙ	25 Ⓐ Ⓑ Ⓒ Ⓓ	35 Ⓕ Ⓖ Ⓗ Ⓙ	45 Ⓐ Ⓑ Ⓒ Ⓓ	55 essay
6 Ⓕ Ⓖ Ⓗ Ⓙ	16 Ⓐ Ⓑ Ⓒ Ⓓ	26 Ⓕ Ⓖ Ⓗ Ⓙ	36 Ⓐ Ⓑ Ⓒ Ⓓ	46 Ⓕ Ⓖ Ⓗ Ⓙ	
7 Ⓐ Ⓑ Ⓒ Ⓓ	17 Ⓕ Ⓖ Ⓗ Ⓙ	27 Ⓐ Ⓑ Ⓒ Ⓓ	37 Ⓕ Ⓖ Ⓗ Ⓙ	47 Ⓐ Ⓑ Ⓒ Ⓓ	
8 Ⓕ Ⓖ Ⓗ Ⓙ	18 Ⓐ Ⓑ Ⓒ Ⓓ	28 Ⓕ Ⓖ Ⓗ Ⓙ	38 Ⓐ Ⓑ Ⓒ Ⓓ	48 Ⓕ Ⓖ Ⓗ Ⓙ	
9 short-answer	19 Ⓕ Ⓖ Ⓗ Ⓙ	29 Ⓐ Ⓑ Ⓒ Ⓓ	39 Ⓕ Ⓖ Ⓗ Ⓙ	49 Ⓐ Ⓑ Ⓒ Ⓓ	
10 short-answer	20 short-answer	30 Ⓕ Ⓖ Ⓗ Ⓙ	40 Ⓐ Ⓑ Ⓒ Ⓓ	50 Ⓕ Ⓖ Ⓗ Ⓙ	